SENSORY SALTATION
Metastability
in the Perceptual World

JOHN M. MacEACHRAN MEMORIAL
LECTURE SERIES, 1975
 (Inaugural Year)

Sponsored by
The Department of Psychology
The University of Alberta
with the support of
The Alma Mater Fund of the University of Alberta
in memory of John M. MacEachran,
pioneer in Canadian psychology.

SENSORY SALTATION

Metastability
in the
Perceptual World

FRANK A. GELDARD

<small>PRINCETON UNIVERSITY</small>

 LAWRENCE ERLBAUM ASSOCIATES,
PUBLISHERS
1975   Hillsdale, New Jersey

DISTRIBUTED BY THE HALSTED PRESS DIVISION OF

JOHN WILEY & SONS

New York   Toronto   London   Sydney

Lawrence Erlbaum Associates, Inc., Publishers
62 Maria Drive
Hillsdale, New Jersey 07642

Distributed solely by Halsted Press Division
John Wiley & Sons, Inc., New York

Library of Congress Cataloging in Publication Data
Geldard, Frank Arthur.
Sensory saltation.

Bibliography: p.
1. Psychology, Physiological.   I. Title.
[DNLM: 1. Perception. 2. Sensation.   3. Neural
transmission.   WL700 G314s]
BF237.G37   152.1   75-22269
ISBN 0-470-29571-6

Printed in the United States of America

Contents

Foreword

No area of experimental psychology can be more closely associated with the historical development of the subject, indeed its very genesis, than that of the study of sensory behavior. In fact, in the very beginning of psychology as a science, sensation was practically synonymous with experimental psychology. However, since the days of Helmholtz and Wundt, few people have managed to maintain impetus and appeal in the area of sensory behavior; today there is little enthusiasm among psychology's young for the study of sensory phenomena. This is at least surprising for several reasons. Certainly the study of the senses lies not only at the very heart of psychology but also is the very foundation of epistemology. A statement made by a famous experimental psychologist some 30 years ago also attests to the usefulness, if not the urgency, of our coming to a better understanding of our sensory systems when he stated that the course of history was decided on the basis of "sensory margin"—where the battle, in this case for democracy, literally depended on the acuities of our human sensory system. This statement is, unfortunately, even more true and vital today and

7

again within a global context. The frightening
pace of technological advancement with its implications for the removal of the human factor has
now been recognized for the paradox it has created. Rather than the removal of the human observer we have placed greater commitments on
his resources. While perhaps freeing him from
many elaborate and wasteful cognitive activities,
we have at the same time tightened the squeeze
by increasing the demands and essentially pushing
sensory capacities as far as they will go. Also, although we have become increasingly aware and
appreciative of the impoverished world of those
suffering from sensory defects, remedial programs
and devices to benefit these individuals can only
be effectively implemented when such programs
and devices reflect an accurate assessment of both
normal and anomalous sensory functioning.

Over the past half century it would be difficult
to think of anyone whose efforts have advanced
our general understanding and appreciation of
sensory behavior more than this year's speaker,
our inaugurator for the MacEachran Memorial
Lecture Series—Frank Geldard.

For the past 40 some years he has maintained
both a scholarly and experimental interest in sensory systems. And I stress the plural, sensory systems. The basic credo of Professor Geldard's pro-
fessional career is succinctly incapsulated in the
preface to the first edition of his book *The Human
Senses*—"the understanding of human nature is
by way of an appreciation of man's senses and

of the fundamental role they play in the attainment of knowledge and the regulation of behavior." J. C. Stevens, in reviewing the second edition of *The Human Senses*, refers to Frank Geldard as a sensory generalist or a sensory impartialist— one who feels at home in psychology, as well as walking comfortably among the senses.

Science progresses not only from the achievements of singular individuals but also from the instruction and example leaders provide to those around them. In reading through several papers presented by students of Professor Geldard at a recent Festschrift in his honor, one theme consistently stands out. Those formally trained in his laboratories at Virginia and Princeton were carefully, yet graciously, nurtured so as to gain a healthy respect and understanding for the experimental method and the "hard facts of psychology," while at the same time developing a genuine enthusiasm for scientific research. We are indeed fortunate in our choice of the inaugural speaker for the MacEachran Memorial Lecture Series.

The realization by the audience that something new and exciting in sensory psychology was being revealed was discerningly voiced by the Chairman of the Department of Psychology, Dr. Thomas M. Nelson, in his concluding remarks:

> There are three things to be said in conclusion. First, I would like to point out what a unique occasion this has been. It has disclosed the existence of entirely new cutaneous, auditory, and visual phenomena that may well be of great importance. Second, I would like to say that these

three lectures have been among the most elucid I have ever attended. Professor Geldard's development of ideas and research strategies are classic. From discovery and phenomenal description he rapidly moves to an exhaustive analysis of stimulation including consideration of time, intensity, spatial distribution, and numerosity. Then he steps to consideration of physiological mechanisms. He starts with local peripheral factors, goes to the neural organization of cutaneous surfaces and thence to the possibility of central factors in cutaneous experience. We conclude only when these are generalized to other modalities using empirical evidence.

Third, I would like to say that I think the lectures were elegant. As one listens to Professor Geldard, thoughts of Faraday's *Chemical History of a Candle* drift into awareness. I do not know how many of you know this little book which represents a series of Christmas lectures delivered by the famous English chemist about 125 years ago. In this book, Faraday combined description, demonstration, observation, and generalization in a way that has provided enduring enjoyment. The whole style was very similar to what we have experienced during the course of this series.

We all realize that this is the first of the MacEachran lectures, and it is important to us that we have a good one. We've got it, and I want to thank Dr. Geldard from the bottom of my heart for a magnificent lecture series.

Finally, and very important, I would like to say to the students that there is another tremendous lesson being taught in this series that has nothing to do with sensory systems whatever. Much of the work reported came to fruition during the last year. The lesson is that it is vigor and firm direction, not circumstance or age, that are the important makings of a scientist.

For the MacEachran Memorial
Lecture Series Committee
E. C. LECHELT, CHAIRMAN

Preface

"Sensory saltation" is a phrase that falls somewhat unfamiliarly on the ear. There should be
little difficulty with "sensory," although its meaning has gotten muddled in recent years by the
widespread obliteration of the sensation–perception distinction, clear to an earlier generation, and
by the revival of the "cognition" category, once
in limbo with much of act psychology but nowa-
days playing conceptual havoc with both "perception" and "sensation." "Saltation" has so little
currency in psychology and related fields as to
make it a real possibility that some fresh meaning
can be injected into it. The word is derived from
the Latin *saltāre* (to dance, leap, or jump) and,
together with about a dozen cognates, has been
with us since at least the late sixteenth century.
It has had meaning as a general action word
("dance," "bound," "leap"), as a technical term
in pathology ("saltatory spasm," a neural condition related to chorea), and as a modern designation in neurology ("saltatory conduction," the
leap of excitation between nodes of Ranvier).
There are some other specific meanings, ranging
from "an order of insects" to "a board game

11

related to checkers"! But we are likely to avoid confusion with any of these, even with the figurative
meaning of "saltation," by which is designated
the departure from orderly and logical progression
in thought. Indeed, we shall be talking of saltation
in quite specific sensory situations, and such a
meaning is not to be found in any dictionary,
ancient or modern.

Very little of the content of this little book is
"off the shelf." Indeed, very little of it is more
than a few years old, for the saltation effect was
discovered, almost serendipitously, as late as 1971.
Had my colleagues and I not been a bit careless
in hooking up some electronic gear it is doubtful
that the "rabbit," with whom we shall get pretty
thoroughly acquainted as we go along, would ever
have come upon the scene at all. But we are getting ahead of our story; this book is really the
biography of a rabbit.

There remains for me to express my appreciation to Professor Thomas M. Nelson, Chairman
of the Department of Psychology at the University
of Alberta, and to Professor Eugene C. Lechelt,
Chairman of its Committee on the MacEachran
Memorial Lecture Series, for the opportunity to
present the lectures on which this book is based
to an audience that through its questions and dis-
cussion proved itself both discerning and con-
genial. For us to have come together to do honor
to a man who left us only a few years ago but
who was a direct academic descendant of Wilhelm
Wundt points up what we knew but have some

difficulty realizing, that psychology, as Hermann Ebbinghaus noted, "has a long past, but only a short history."

I have been in psychology almost exactly fifty years, and when I tell students that, among other memorable contacts, my first scientific paper was read in the presence of E. B. Titchener, that I was an active pallbearer at the funeral of G. Stanley Hall, and that I served a summer apprenticeship, while still a graduate student, with Joseph Jastrow, they have been known to ask, "Did you know Wundt, too?" The question is not nearly as absurd as, at first blush, it appears: Wundt died just the year before I entered the University. We are still getting psychology established as a science and are having unconscionable growing pains doing it.

It is a signal honor for me to have been invited to initiate the MacEachran Memorial Lecture Series. I wish for it a long and influential life, like that of Professor MacEachran himself.

Finally, I should like here to record my indebtedness to the U.S. National Institutes of Health. Through their Grant NS-04755 to Princeton University they have provided both the wherewithal and the freedom to complete the experimental work reported in this book.

I

The Concept of Metastability

Many years ago an old friend whom I greatly admired and respected wrote a little book carrying the intriguing title, *Ghosts I have talked with* (McComas, 1935). The author, Henry McComas of the Johns Hopkins University, designed the book to be essentially an exposé of psychological quacks and charlatans, chiefly in and around Baltimore, whose "services" he and his close friend, Knight Dunlap, had engaged in the course of many weekend visits to practicing fortune tellers, clairvoyants, and other advertising occultists. The adventurous pair had run the spiritistic gamut, and the book coming out of their experiences provided both amusing and engrossing reading. In putting together the story of the experiments that are to engage us throughout this series of lectures I have been tempted to paraphrase the McComas attention-getting title and label these chapters *Ghosts I have lived with,* or some such, even though there is not so much as a whisper of charlatanry in the topics that concern us here.

For the past several years my colleagues and I have been dealing with phenomena involving illusory localizations of sensations, with things that are where they should not be, with appearances that do not coincide with the rules of order in the physical, geometric world. In short, we have been living with ghosts and phantoms that, although in no sense imaginary, just do not show up in the right place in the experienced world.

But what is the "right place"? Why should we have firm expectations as to the "where" of things? The answer is not hard to find. In a workaday world we must trust our senses; we come to view the world as "out there," substantial, real. The senses we rely on most commonly for our welfare, the so-called distance senses of vision and audition (and, considerably less frequently, olfaction), bring that world to us "as it is." Most of the time we raise no question as to the reality of the outside world—events progress in an orderly manner, satisfying most of our expectations—and if occasionally there appears a discrepancy in which some of the details of our ordered world fail to check precisely with what we know about temporal and spatial relations in that world, especially if a checkup with the body-bound sense of touch confirms the discrepancy, then we say we are subject to illusion.

The frequency with which illusion is upon us is not ordinarily appreciated. Indeed, one cannot go far into the study of human perception without making the important discovery that illusion, not veridicality, is the rule. All sense channels are normally subject to illusion, both with respect to time and space. Think of the generality with which the common geometrical illusions must intervene in our everyday experience. Straight lines are invariably overestimated with respect to length; circles or portions of them are underestimated in size. Where lines intersect, unless they do so at right angles, there is invariably an overestimation or underestimation of the angle, depending on whether it is acute or obtuse. Squares can become oblongs, straight lines can appear bent or curved, circles become distorted in outline, and the third dimension can be wrung inside out, all depending on the context in which these elements appear. Some illusions seem to depend heavily on past experience to set the stage. We are sometimes led into perceptual error through habits of attending and observing, although, as the Gestalt psychologists have quite correctly pointed out, when explanations are being sought for novel perceptual appearances passing them off as "the result of past experience" is indulged in by psychologists much too readily.

The vital role played by impoverishment of sensory cues in producing distortions of reality is evident in several well-known perceptual phenomena. Perhaps the most extensive alteration comes about when the supporting framework is taken away from a relatively unstructured visual object, as in the familiar autokinetic effect. Let a small, isolated point of light be viewed continuously against darkness and there comes to be generated, after a time, a series of gliding, wandering, and jerky movements, even rapid swooping of the light through space. This phenomenon, well known in aviation circles, unquestionably has been responsible for more than one fatal accident. A pilot, holding too steady fixation on the wing light of his squadron leader in night flight, suddenly sees a rapid deviation of flight path as in the maneuver known as a "wingover," attempts to follow, and finds himself in a collision course with another aircraft. He either crashes into it or goes into a dangerous spin. The hazards of the autokinetic phenomenon are so well recognized in flight training as to be responsible for the oft-repeated admonition to "keep the eyes moving," glued neither to instruments or external small objects, especially points of light against darkness. In an earlier time, during World War I, the autokinetic effect was the underlying cause of the not infrequent rumors that German Zeppelins were attacking the Rocky Mountain regions. Presumably steady gaze on a distant mountainside cabin light gave the impression of a hovering dirigible; presumably it is also true that any number of contemporary reports of UFOs may be traced to the same autokinetic source.

A step up the scale of complication leads to the consideration of another perceptual illusion, also one with practical if less dangerous consequences. The so-called "reduction screen" of experimental psychology demonstrates it. Hold an ordinary mailing tube to the eye while viewing a uniformly colored surface. What starts out as a flat plane seen at a fixed distance shortly changes to an unsubstantial colored cloud filling up the end of the tube. If illumination is even and there are no visible details to testify that the color path actually belongs to a surface, the filmy texture of the color is quite undeniable. Which is the reality?

Another prime illustration, also representative of some degree of complication both in its phenomenal appearance and in its practical consequences, is that of the so-called oculogyral illusion. Under angular acceleration in a human centrifuge a subject views against darkness a dim star pattern of six radial lines. During acceleration the lines visibly drift in the direction of turn. When the machine levels off at a uniform velocity, visual movement stops, then later resumes in the opposite direction under subsequent deceleration. The physical change in velocity of the centrifuge can be as little as one-tenth of a degree per second per second for the oculogyral illusion to put in its appearance. Indeed, this channel of reporting speedups and slowdowns of bodily motion is the most sensitive one we possess for this function, more sensitive by far than the subject's own impressions of his movement. The mechanism of the illusion's operation is, of course, slight reflex nystagmic deflections of the eyes prompted by tiny displacements of the fluid of the inner ear labyrinth—a complex sequence of events, indeed.

This brief parade of visual illusions has been conducted with the purpose in mind of demonstrating the profound fact of perceptual life that illusion is very general and intervenes in our every experience with the external world. A review of auditory perceptions would similarly yield evidences of illusion. The difference is that, whereas the illusory phenomena we have to deal with in vision are mainly spatial, audition, which for the most part deals only indirectly and in a derived way with space, is a past master with time and with generating temporal judgments. The ear's traffic with space is pretty much confined to orientation cues, but its mediation of noise, speech, and music is everywhere related to frequency and rhythm, basic manifestations of time.

And so one must conclude, as a firmly fixed scientific generalization, that the properties of the external world are rarely represented in a straightforward way in the human responses triggered by energies in that world. Should perception therefore be expected to be disorganized and chaotic? Not at all. A psychophysics that looked for exact correspondences between the dimensions of psychology and the dimensions of physics would be a simple-minded science indeed. The psychophysics of hearing, for example, is largely written in terms of the four psychological dimensions of pitch, loudness, volume, and density. These come to be related to the physical dimensions of wave frequency and amplitude—only these two are needed—yet no single psychological dimension is simply related to a physical one. Pitch is primarily dependent on frequency but somewhat on amplitude. Loudness depends more directly on amplitude but is also a function of frequency. So too for volume and density; they are more nearly balanced joint functions of frequency and amplitude. Similar, although even more elaborate, relations are found in vision and, indeed, they are probably discoverable in all sense channels. Moreover, they shall be if we ever reach the point where stimulus attributes are precisely describable in terms of energetics throughout the whole sensory realm.

The reason for the apparent disjunction between external stimulus properties and those of the final percept is not hard to find. The physiological organism, standing between these two end terms, has dimensions of its own to contribute, makes its own transformations, and creates its own nonlinear functional relationships in the devious paths from peripheral receptor processes to final response mechanism.

There is a more fundamental consideration than any yet voiced. Scientists have staunch faith in the principle of the uniformity of nature. Events repeat themselves. Whenever conditions identical with those that have evoked a phenomenon are reinstated, the phenomenon is highly likely to recur. This is what is expected of the particles of physics, the genes of genetics, and the planets in their courses, and it is no less the expectation that man's sense organs and nervous system perform similarly. Perceptual experience, although intricately organized, is predictable if enough is known about the conditions nurturing it.

All this leads to an important generalization, to wit, that perceptual experience, despite its proneness to illusion at every turn, despite the complexity of the chain of events linking it with the outside world, is essentially stable. Visual objects are, by and large, what they seem to be; they have a predictable appearance with respect to size, shape, color, and brightness provided only that one knows the prior state of adaptation of the visual system and can fill in the specifics of the physical and physiological changes taking place en route to nervous centers. Indeed, another somewhat mysterious influence, collectively called "constancy," sweeps away any threatening discrepancies between prediction and realization and further stabilizes experience by allowing visual objects to preserve their accustomed size, shape, color, brightness, and even distance.

Somewhat comparable things happen in the realm of hearing, especially at levels involving the complex frequency aggregations of speech and music. Think of the number and variety of onslaughts that can be made on the speech signal without really seriously degrading intelligibility. Peak clipping, for example, may be made to reduce the voice signal by as much as 94% of its original amplitude and the result will be only a 5% decline in the intelligibility of monosyllabic words (Licklider & Miller, 1951). Vocal communication is only a little hampered when speech sounds are rapidly and continuously interrupted so that they are turned off as much as half the time. Conversation is still intelligible when either the upper or the lower half of the speech spectrum is obliterated, when serious phase distortion is introduced, or when masking interference is supplied in substantial amounts; and there are other adverse circumstances that the speech signal can resist. In short, the auditory sense, like vision, is a stable sense. Throughout its billion-to-one power range, from the faintest whisper to the most energetic shout, from the faintest threshold flutter of the tympanic membrane to the dangerous blast 120 or more decibels up the scale, it reflects with some fidelity the ever-changing and intricate world of sound.

What of the chemical senses, smell and taste? Except in a primitive way, these modalities have next to nothing to do with the immediate appreciation of either space or time. Certainly, the occasions are rare when one attempts to orient oneself by sniffing, although some ingenious experiments by von Békésy (1967) demonstrate that the mechanism of localization is far from lacking in this sense. Moreover, competent observation puts a volumic property into taste sensations. And there is, of course, the matter of bare extensity and protensity in both smell and taste; we have been led to believe that no sensation can survive the reduction to zero of either of these dimensions. Despite all this it is too harsh a judgment to say that the chemical senses are basically unstable. They display highly reproducible qualities, even if there is a good deal of confusion between the two as to which channel is reporting which. Moreover, they enjoy   the same kind of predictability we have encountered in vision and hearing.

There are some odd happenings, however, odd in the sense that in a stable sensory system one would not suppose things to work the way they do. It is perfectly predictable that solutions having an excess of free hydrogen ions are going to taste sour; it is less obvious that table salt, in the just suprathreshold region, should taste sweet rather than salty, which it does at higher concentrations. In olfaction it is predictable that α- and β-ionone, which differ chemically from each other only with respect to where double bonds appear in their ring structure, should greatly resemble each other in odor. Both are used to produce the violet smell in perfume. Why should it be, then, that rather complete exhaustion of sensitivity to one of these, in adaptation experiments (Moncrieff, 1956), leaves the other relatively unaffected? Why should close chemical relatives not display family traits? The proper conclusion may be that we have a lot to learn about such matters. I doubt that the conclusion should be that the chemical senses are either fickle or unstable.

Quite intentionally I have left until last any consideration of the sense of feeling, for I wish to move it to the center of the stage, not only for this chapter but for the next one as well. The relative stability of the major senses has been stressed and, for the chemical senses, it has seemed more reasonable to conclude for our ignorance than for any inherent instability. Now, approaching touch and the other somesthetic senses, let us make a preliminary judgment that here we must deal with a perceptual mediator that is less than fully stable in many of its manifestations, that, in fact, is characterized by relative instability. Indeed, I should like to apply a term borrowed from physics and chemistry, where it signifies "precarious stability" or "delicate equilibrium" and is commonly applied to easily decomposed compounds, atmospheric changes, supercooled liquids, and the like. The term is "metastability" and if it does not fall familiarly on the ear, I shall endeavor to inject some meaning into it. My thesis shall be that in many tactile phenomena we are dealing with evidences for what is essentially a metastable sense. This is not to imply that all instances of metastability occur in somesthesis. On the contrary, we have already encountered a prime instance of it in vision—the autokinetic effect. Neither is it difficult to find an auditory example. A case in point is the modulation effect described by von Békésy (1962) in which a high-frequency tone (5000 Hz) is modulated 100% by a very low one (10 Hz). As intensity is increased the modulation frequency produces a low-pitched tone that progressively lowers until, at 60-dB sensation level, it has a pitch over an octave lower than where it started: metastable, indeed. Unmodulated tones also show a little lack of stability. It has long been known that tones above about 1300 Hz show a rise in pitch on being loudened, whereas those below this balance point suffer a lowering of pitch as they are augmented in loudness. Fortunately, this happens only with pure tones, not those of complex timbre such as occur in music. It would be disconcerting, to say the least, if your favorite symphony orchestra were to veer off pitch during crescendos and diminuendos!

Actually, if you heard with your skins such would happen, and this circumstance provides a good opportunity to enter on our consideration of cutaneous metastability. Indeed, we can look at the cutaneous analog of the loudened tone experiment. Let a relatively low-frequency vibration, 40 Hz, say, be supplied to the fingertip, the observer being instructed to attend to the rate or "pitch" of the vibration as it is "loudened" or "softened." (Note the way in which those of us working in somesthesis have to steal auditory descriptive terms to deal with the very fundamentals of the sensations we are investigating; sensations originating in the skin are so little attended to that we have never devised a proper language for them). Now, leaving the frequency control undisturbed, let the amplitude of vibration be increased—slowly or rapidly, it does not matter. The observer invariably reports that pitch has gone down. Lighten up on amplitude and he says that pitch has risen. The engineer may say that here we are dealing with a tradeoff relation between frequency and amplitude. Very well, we are, but additionally I can say that we have *prima facie* evidence for metastability in the somesthetic sphere.

A metastable state is also revealed in another phenomenon having to do with vibrotactile sensation. Perceived loudness or vibration on the skin is found to be a joint function of amplitude and frequency, as in hearing. If a vibrating contactor is continuously brought up in amplitude at, say, a frequency of 250 Hz (the point of maximal sensitivity, corresponding to 3000 Hz in audition), the gently whirring feeling at threshold grows into a smooth buzzing, which shows a rapid rise in loudness, and ultimately this gives way to a powerful "pounding." Much beyond this point there is outright discomfort, perhaps even damage to tissues, and this should not be surprising when it is considered that a miniature triphammer is assaulting the skin 250 times a second. The interesting question is: where is this point of discomfort on the intensity scale? Is it in the neighborhood of 110–120 dB, as in hearing? Far from it. It is no higher than 60 dB above threshold, a value in hearing corresponding to the average loudness of ordinary social conversation. Actually, most vibratory experiments on the skin are conducted at intensities ranging from a few decibels to 15–20 dB, the whisper range for hearing. Something less than a comfortable level for most skin areas is reached at around 35 dB.

What is the lesson for metastability in all this? Simply that, as compared with audition at least, the sense of feeling is responding in a very badly controlled fashion. As the energy imparted to the system is increased, loudness jumps ahead by disproportionate leaps and bounds. The analogous behavior in hearing is the response characteristic of a partially nerve-deaf ear. The skin appears to "recruit" like one and thus evinces its metastability.

What has turned out to be the best evidence yet for metastability involves a phenomenon, utterly new as far as we know, that was encountered quite unexpectedly. One should hesitate before making the claim of novelty for any scientific observation and it is always hazardous to aver, as so many introductory paragraphs of journal articles do, that no one has ever done such-and-such. One remembers the admonition of a literature search bureau of some years ago to the effect that "more is known than is known is known" and realization of this tends to put down arrogance. In this instance, however, all attempts to link our find with the past only confirm its apparent freshness.

What is the effect in question? Let us consider a simple cutaneous stimulation situation. Three identical contactors are placed about 4 inches apart on the forearm (Figure 1). Each is capable of delivering a sequence of sharp taps, being energized by square waves of only a few milliseconds duration. Now let the three contactors be put into operation sequentially, each in turn receiving five rapid pulses and with no pause in passing from

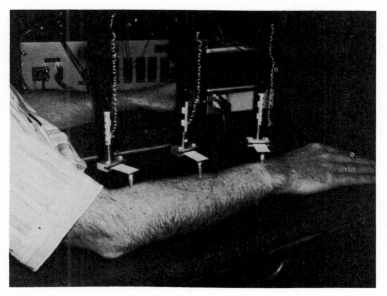

FIGURE 1. The three contactors, driven by Bimorph benders, in place on the dorsal forearm. Static pressure is controlled by the tubular spring dynamometers which, in turn, are suspended from the ceiling to minimize "crosstalk" among the vibrators.

one vibrator to the next. In the right range of repetition rates—and this can be anything from 5 to
50 pulses per second, optimally about 20—instead
of feeling three well-spaced bursts located under
the contactors, the 15 taps appear to distribute
themselves uniformly from the region of the first
contactor to that of the third. There is a slow,
sweeping movement punctuated by taps. The impression is that of a tiny rabbit hopping up the
arm. Indeed, we began calling it "the rabbit" and
the name persisted, I suppose because of the plea-
sant imagery connected with it. We had the
temerity, Dr. Carl Sherrick and I (Geldard & Sherrick, 1972), to publish a little paper in the weekly
journal, *Science,* describing the antics of our new-
found friend, and used the word "rabbit" in the
title. Had we anticipated the answering of reprint
requests from zoological institutes and such we
should perhaps have chosen a different designation. As it is, we have subsequently come to adopt
the term, "saltation," which may detract from the
vivid appeal of our woodland friend but also dig-
nifies him to a degree. Unless you find it disconcerting, I shall continue to refer to him as "the
rabbit"; like that redoubtable pooka in "Harvey,"
he has become one of the family (Figure 2).

We shall be living with the rabbit from here
on out; it is well, therefore, to ask why the phenomenon he represents is being linked with metastability. The answer is that localization anomalies
of the kind found in touch are perhaps the most
extreme instances of the upsetting of "delicate

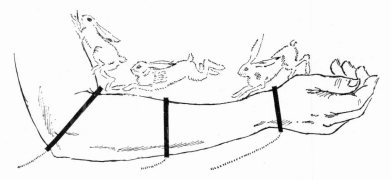

FIGURE 2.   One conception of the "rabbit," supplied by a Norwegian newspaper cartoonist.

equilibria," of the existence of "precarious stability," to be found anywhere in sensory psychophysiology. Mainly for this reason we have been assiduously prying into the various properties of the saltation effect, not only asking "What makes the rabbit run?" but "What manner of creature is he?" and "What conditions will alter his behavior?"

It is not proposed at this time to go deeply into the many experiments that have been performed on the saltation phenomenon over the span of the last three years. We shall have a careful look at some of them in the second and third chapters. However, we do need to get generally familiar with the main manifestations of the phenomenon. We need to know both the necessary and sufficient conditions of their arousal. I propose to raise and answer, at least tentatively, a series of questions by way of providing a preview.

1. What history does the phenomenon have? We have said, somewhat categorically, that there is none, so far as we know. However, the sophisticate may say—and many have—that the tactual phi phenomenon must be at the root of the matter. Tactual "phi" is not exactly an unknown, even though it has not been investigated with anything like the thoroughness of visual "phi." After all, perceived movement provided the platform from which there was launched a whole modern school of psychology. Are we simply failing to recognize the occurrence of synthetic tactual movement of the "phi" variety? The answer is no, definitely not. Phi movement is also present, along with the rabbit, when times, intensities, and distances are right for it and it is easily recognized when it is present. Phi movement, however, is a gray ghost compared to the rabbit. The heart of the saltation effect is its discontinuity and discreteness. The taps created between stimulus loci are separate and distinct. One can point to them. The rabbit is a *Ding an sich.*

The other feature of the phenomenon's history that may be worth recounting is what has been referred to above as its serendipitous aspect. It was a lucky accident that brought the phenomenon to light. We were intent on repeating, with modern electronic equipment, a provocative tactual experiment, unfortunately too little known, in which there had been demonstrated a time–space interaction. This was the work of Helson and King (1931) on the so-called "tau effect." We had planned to deliver to three spaced vibrators, arrayed on the dorsal forearm, sinusoidal waves of varying duration, exact timing to be supplied by the punched tape of the Tally reader. Through an inadvertence the wrong source was plugged in; instead of smooth buzzes on our vibrators, a succession of sharp, well-spaced square waves was supplied. To the observer's astonishment, rather than the three prolonged buzzes he expected, there came a clear train of sharp taps running up the arm. Instead of a report on two neighboring spatial intervals, his reaction took

more nearly the form, "Who let the rabbit loose?"
Instead of three spaced buzzes he had felt a succession of tiny hops sweeping up the forearm,
some at contactor sites, some scattered between
them. It was a startling experience, one repeated
hundreds of times since with very little attenua-
tion of the original wonderment. The saltatory
effect, unrecognized because unknown, had
sprung, almost Athene-like, from the forearm of
Zeus!

Why previously unknown? We must not be the
only laboratory making lucky experiments; indeed,
we can think of several that deserve to have such
things happen in their precincts. However, to arrange for multiple taps on each of several linearly
disposed contactors activated in train seems an
unlikely undertaking. Such an experimental plan
does not emerge naturally from any conventional
or familiar hypothesis in somesthesis.

The "tau" experiment of Helson and King
seems to have derived its inspiration from earlier
work, some visual, some tactual, that had more
than a little influence on *Gestalt-theorie*. The experiments of Benussi (1916) and those of Gelb
(1914) are in point. But neither appears to have
found the rabbit. Nor did Burtt (1917), whose
array of tactual stimulators in his extensive study
of synthetic movement might easily have supplied
the opportunity for its discovery. Indeed, Burtt's
observers came very close to talking about it. His
approach was to arrange a linear series of brass
contactors actuated by solenoids. Normally, these

were positioned in a row 1 mm above the dorsal surface of the forearm. Two or more contactors being presented successively, the synthetic motion was noted and immediately compared with that given by a series of ten closely spaced contactors, which were energized successively in a single sweep. The ten were intended to provide "real" movement. To quote Burtt: "The [illusory] movement impression was variously characterized in the introspection of the subjects. . . . [One observer] noted . . . a walk in which there are a number of discrete points in succession. . . . [Another observer] reported movement in which they 'skip along like playing four or five notes on a piano in succession.' It often suggested a little boy running along [p. 375]."

It was doubtless supposed by Burtt that, in rapidly making and breaking a dc current to the solenoids (through the intervention of a Leipzig "time sense" apparatus) he was simply applying a single brief "tap" to the skin surface. Actually, experiment shows that application of a brief square-wave pulse to the coil of a solenoid such as was used in this experiment results in not a single tap but at least a double one. With a "current-on" duration of 10 msec or more, with a relatively sluggish solenoid of the type Burtt employed, and with the skin damping out accessory oscillations, Dr. Carl Sherrick, who knows this situation well (Sherrick, 1968, p. 334), estimates that two successive stimuli generated in this manner probably behave "as a quartet or as a double

trio of events." Burtt's exposure times vary between 15 and 160 msec; it is therefore not surprising that commonly recurring reports in his tables
are of "3 or 4 in succession" and "discrete groups
walking." Burtt presumably had encountered the
rabbit but was not in the best position to recognize
him; he mistook the pooka for a little boy! It was,
of course, easier for us. We knew how many pulses
ought to be there and what they should do. When
three long buzzes became 15 sharp taps considerably more than a just noticeable difference was
embraced. Burtt's observers had much more to
contend with.

   *2. Is there an optimal number of contactors and
pulses?*   The number of contactors seems not to
be crucial except where extraordinary distances
are to be spanned. There must, of course, be at
least two, and we happen to have had three in
the prototype experiment. We shall return to this
question later.

   The number of pulses delivered to any one contactor is a more important variable, although there
is a wide range over which successful saltation
can be achieved provided proper timing is employed. As few as two pulses per contactor can
yield the spaced hops, and as many as 15 pulses
on each contactor, a total of 45, can do the same.
The temporal spacing has to be quite different in
the two instances. Moreover, the 45-pulse rabbit
takes mincing steps, the six-pulse variety takes
broad leaps. More than about 15 taps per contactor, at least with any repetition rates obtainable

by us (and we can go to nearly 60 per second without special arrangements), leads to a breakdown of the hopping. The taps tend to get "anchored" under the contactors when the train persists that long in one place.

It is of some interest to observe the initial displacement of the hops away from a contactor site. Taking as a standard stimulating situation a lineup of three contactors on the dorsal forearm, 10 cm apart, and with a five-pulse train of 2-msec pulses on each, one may begin by using a relatively long interpulse interval, 400 msec, say. The total of 15 pulses is felt where they "belong," that is, five under each contactor. Now, shorten the interstimulus interval progressively. In the neighborhood of 250 msec between pulses, on close observation there are found to be stirrings under the first and second contactors and quite promptly this becomes a pronounced "scattering" of taps. Very shortly it will be noted that a definite localization error is present; then there will come the realization that a perceptible hopping into the intercontactor space has occurred. The point at which the taps just begin to escape the contactor area we have dubbed "exodus," for this is where the rabbit is just emerging.

As the interpulse interval is further shortened below the exodus point the taps display "hops" and ultimately "leaps." The hopping is in evidence at around 100–125 msec and well-distributed and vivid leaping characteristically occur at between 40 and 60 msec. There are some other variables that can alter these figures, but we are speaking not too precisely about commonly encountered conditions.

With further shortening of the interstimulus interval the apparent number of taps begins to shrink until, at the most rapid rates (about 20 msec between pulses), the total of 15 may seem to have reduced to five or six. This phenomenon elicits no surprise in those interested in experiments on numerosity and numerousness.

3. Are there limitations on the phenomenon imposed by bodily distance, direction, or locus of stimulation? To some degree these must be dealt with separately. Locus apparently is of little consequence; we have never encountered a failure, and we have explored the body pretty thoroughly. Direction likewise imposes no restriction. The rabbit can leap down the arm, leg, or trunk, as readily as it can go up. Indeed, both things can be made to occur simultaneously. If, for example, five vibrators are disposed on the forearm in a lineal array and the middle (Contactor 3) is energized first, then Contactors 2 and 4 simultaneously, then Contactors 1 and 5, also simultaneously, the hopping occurs in both directions at the same time (Figure 3). Reversing the order brings about a collision of rabbits, and this arouses some interesting imagery. One tender-hearted observer reported that the two veered away from each other just before the moment of impact!

The matter of distance may well be crucial for an understanding of saltation. Successful continuity of jumps may be had at both long and short

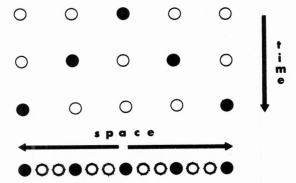

FIGURE 3. Successive stimulation from two directions. Spatial relations are represented horizontally,
temporal ones vertically. Sequences are described in
text.

distances. On the arm the effect may be demonstrated for distances ranging from 2 to 35 cm.
When five contactors have been distributed so as
to have one on each forearm, one on each upper
arm, and the fifth on the nape of the neck, sequen-
tial energizing of the vibrators with trains of five
pulses each has caused the rabbit to run up one
arm, across the shoulders, and down the other
arm.

In one experiment a total of six contactors was
arrayed over a distance of 150 cm, from ankle to
shoulder on one side of the body. There was no
difficulty in getting good, continuous leaping patterns. However, when every other contactor was
silenced and the temporal gaps were closed up,
the rabbit failed to appear. Apparently, the distance limit had been transcended. In this same experiment use of any three contiguous contactors
reinstated the saltatory pattern.

4. *What happens with irregular pulsing?* If
something other than equal temporal spacing is
introduced, skipping one or more beats, overlap-
ping the sequences in different vibrators, producing syncopated rhythms, etc., there are necessarily
complications. Up to a point, however, our furry
friend tolerates such departures from orderliness.
The omission of a single pulse in a 15-pulse series
is promptly noticed but a speeding of the train
of pulses restores distinctness. Two successive
blank intervals, at least at some speeds, do not
destroy the overall effect but may induce an easily

perceived rhythm in it. Apparently the skipping of three or four is impossible to bridge, and the saltatory effect is totally destroyed. There has not as yet been any systematic attack on this question; the topic of tolerable gap lengths under various conditions merits study.

5. *Is the saltation phenomenon susceptible to alteration by "tuning" or preconditioning?* There seem to be some possibilities here, although it should be said straightway that no preliminaries are required in calling forth the effect. Some perceptual phenomena, such as the apparent tilting of the visual field in aniseikonia, various of the tridimensional effects described by Julesz (1971), and MacKay's (1961) extraordinary rotary "brain motion" phenomenon—to mention only a few of the most vivid appearances that have led to recent excitement—seem to require a period of buildup, one of development through time. Not so with the rabbit; given the conditions already described, the hops come out promptly. However, it also appears that temporal spacing too slow to yield what may be termed a "good" rabbit, that is, one having well-distributed hops, can become effective if preceded by repetitive rapid sequences lasting 30 sec or so. Conversely, inhibition of the effect can be brought about by reversing the direction of the "preconditioning" stimulus. It appears that there is something of an inertial property here, also one that deserves more attention than it has yet received.

6. What are the minimum essentials for the production of saltation? It should be apparent by now that the saltatory effect has been both discovered and initially worked on in a state of considerable complication. Three or more contactors are not needed for it, nor are long trains of pulses. It became obvious quite early that, if we were going to penetrate to the underlying mechanism actuating the rabbit, the approach would have to be more analytical. Some simplification was needed.

A first step consists in reducing the number of contactors to two. If this is done it is found that the second vibrator need have supplied to it no more than one pulse; regularly spaced hops will still result. A single well-timed tap at a second locus, which we may now call the "attractant," is sufficient to affect a whole train of taps at the first locus. If two attractants are provided at different loci, the initial train of hops will be replicated in the second path. If there are four attractants positioned in different directions, there will arise four sets of hops diverging from each other.

Obviously, still greater simplification can be achieved. The "attractee," so to speak, need not have five or more pulses. Although overall vividness suffers, jumping can be had with fewer, even with only one. What we are now saying is that a localization anomaly can be created if no more than two spatially and temporally separated impressions are produced in the skin.

One of the difficulties of such a thorough reduction of conditions to a single pulse on each of two contactors is that the lack of repetition leads to general disorientation in the localizing task. This difficulty may be surmounted quite easily, however. It is only necessary to precede the tap at the first locus (the "attractee") by another, localizing tap. If the new one is sufficiently spaced out in time it does not interact with the other.

This, then, is what has been done in our experiments. What we have called the "reduced rabbit" (Figure 4) consists of a three-pulse sequence: (1) a localizing pulse, which simply indicates to the observer where the first locus is; (2) a second pulse, also at the first locus (the "attractee"); and (3) a third pulse, appearing at the second locus (the "attractant"). Variable time intervals between the second and third pulses yield predictable localization shifts. We shall be hearing much more about the reduced rabbit, for it proves to be a valuable analytic device, performing much the same service for cutaneous sensibility as the "reduced eye" of Listing, which helps solve many dioptric problems by presenting a simple set of lines that are geometrically correct but that avoid the many complexities of the true path of light through the optic media (Donders, 1864).

7. *Can anything of practical importance be expected of saltatory induction?* There are several classic answers to this question of the utility of scientific findings. They range from Faraday's retort to the inquiry as to what might be done with his induction motor ("Maybe you can tax it some day") to Franklin's quip in response to the question, "What good is it?" ("What good is a

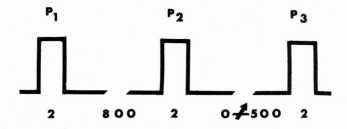

P_1 P_2 P_3

2   800   2   0—500   2

T I M E   (m s e c)

FIGURE 4. Time relations in the "reduced" rabbit. P_1 is a 2-msec localizing pulse preceding P_2 by 800 msec; P_2 is the "attractee," the pulse that gets systematically displaced, depending on the time interval between P_2 and P_3; P_3 is the "attractant" and typically has a veridical localization. Both P_1 and P_2 occur physically at the first locus, L_1; P_3 is delivered to the second locus, L_2.

44

baby?"). Whether the rabbit can be harnessed for useful work is a query the answer to which lies well into the future. Meanwhile, we do have high hopes for it as a possible element in cutaneous communication systems for the blind and deaf. At least, we are encouraged by preliminary experiments, one with a nine-vibratory matrix, another with a larger matrix employing 16 bimorph benders. If single pulses are delivered successively to each of an array of vibrators forming the contour of the letter "O," say, there is no possibility, at any temporal spacing, of synthesizing a recognizable shape from it. Tactual "phi" just does not work this way. However, put a short train of pulses on each vibrator and follow the same path, and the synthetic contour comes out strongly. It is obvious that here we have a novel form of graphesthesia and one that may well turn out to be most useful. At any rate, we now have under construction a 64-element matrix that can be activated by a computer capable of delivering any desired pattern and temporal spacing, and there are high expectations of its providing a range of intelligible signals.

This preview has touched on the most important general questions, even though these are not the only ones that can be asked. A myriad of manipulations can be entered into with sensory saltation. So far there has been time and effort for something less than myriad answers.

II

Somesthetic Saltation

With some of the general properties of the saltation effect now before us, we are in a stronger position to appreciate the results of manipulating the conditions surrounding its appearance. The best approach to any little understood phenomenon is first to identify the variables present and then, in a controlled fashion, to change its parameters over as wide a range as can be tolerated. Such an attack lets us know which variables matter, which ones do not. Only by making such systematic assessment does one come by the stuff of which hypotheses are made, only by setting up hypotheses can meaningful experiments be devised, and only by performing the right experiments can durable facts come into our possession.

The whole point, it will be recalled, in reducing to their simplest terms the conditions that produce saltation is to make the leaping eminently observable, to permit a judgment of the extent of the leaping without contamination or distraction. Let us reconstruct the experimental situation. Figure 5 represents not only the Bimorph benders, mounted on their spring dynamometers to control static skin pressure, but the time course of the pulses

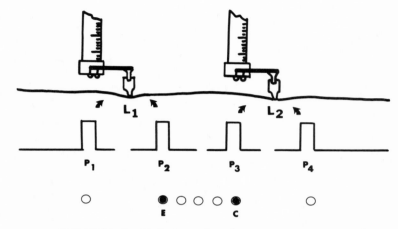

FIGURE 5. Relation of pulses to contactors and loci of stimulation. P_1 and P_4 are purely localizing pulses and are so far separated in time from P_2 and P_3, respectively, as not to affect tap localization. Long intervals between P_2 and P_3 result in veridical localization (E), short ones produce saltation, with maximal leaping at C.

that energize them. P_1, a localizing pulse coming 800 msec in advance of P_2, does not enter the saltatory reaction because of the large time gap between it and P_2. The second pulse, P_2, does do so, of course. Indeed, it is the principal actor in the saltatory drama. It is the "attractee," the tap that leaps out of position when the time is right and occupies an apparent position somewhere between the two loci of stimulation (L_1 and L_2). P_1 and P_2 are both delivered to L_1. P_2 may also be found emerging from L_1 if the interval between P_2 and P_3 is relatively long. This is "exodus." Or it may appear at or near L_2 if P_3, the "attractant," is sufficiently strong and the time is short enough. The appearance of P_2 in the L_2 position, that is, a leap covering the whole distance between stimulators, is called "coincidence." Strictly speaking, coincidence, like exodus, receives the psychophysical definition accorded thresholds. It is the extent of time that will just noticeably permit P_2 to emerge from under L_2, or as we are being precise, will do so 75% of the time. As a practical matter, because the P_3 pulse creates its own tap at L_2, coincidence is best judged by noting the changes in loudness and spatial pattern that occur in the L_2 region.

There we have the important elements of the reduced rabbit: a preliminary tap at L_1 that says "Here is the place"; a second tap that roves between L_1 and L_2, depending on the time interval between P_2 and P_3; and a third tap, ordinarily found where it is delivered, at L_2. Having said that

P_3 appears where it belongs, it must be hastily added that in some experiments the instability of the P_3 tap has seemed to be such that a marker has had to be provided at L_2, a P_4 tap performing a duty similar to that of P_1. P_4 was spaced out 800 msec after P_3, and occasionally P_4 and P_3 seemed not to coincide exactly. However, the overall conclusion about P_4 is that it is, by and large, a supernumerary, no regular or systematic deviations at L_2 having come to light through its use. We shall largely drop it from consideration in what is to come.

Now, familiar with the structure of the reduced rabbit, we are in a position to look into what can be done with it. It was obvious in early observations that quantification of the extent of the jumps could come from comparisons with synthetic movement induced on the opposite side of the body. In one experiment, for example, six contactors were arrayed from wrist to shoulder on the left arm. These were equally spaced, and to each there was delivered a single brief pulse. Through the operation of the tactual "phi" effect there was induced a continuous sweep, punctuated by the six taps, that traveled from wrist to shoulder. On the right arm there were distributed three contactors, also extending over nearly the same total distance, and these were given two taps each. Timing was then adjusted to yield the same apparent spacing as that obtaining on the left arm. When the patterns on the two arms were alternately compared they were judged to be equivalent. Besides reaffirming the reality of the saltation effect, which this experiment does handsomely, there is also revealed a possible technique for measuring the extent of the leaps. It would only be necessary to adjust the spacing of the veridical hops to match the observed magnitude of the saltatory ones. Actually, this method was not put into service extensively. Instead, it was found that with the lesser complication of the reduced rabbit other ways of assessing the size of the leap could be found.

With the reduced rabbit in effect on one arm it is possible to point with some accuracy to the apparent position of P_2. This was done at first with a simple stylus immediately following each trial. Then, greater precision was attained by using a movable bimorph, a duplicate of those at L_1 and L_2, that could be set down promptly where the P_2 tap had just been felt. Correction was allowed if, on first placement, the third bimorph's tap did not square with the lingering impression of the P_2 phantom. This procedure, of course, simulates that traditionally employed in single-point tactual localization experiments. At least, it simulates one of the procedures; Professor Boring (1942, p. 484) has calculated there to be 121 ways of doing that experiment!

Both these techniques proved effective, but so did a simpler one, viz., one in which the observer, without performing a comparison of any kind, made an estimate of the relative portion of the distance between L_1 and L_2 over which the leap had occurred. Indeed, it was now possible to put in the hands of the observer control of the time interval between P_2 and P_3, what we shall henceforth refer to as the $(P_3 - P_2)$ interval. We require him to make a suitable adjustment on a multiturn potentiometer to bring the hop first to exodus; then successively to three nodal points, the one-quarter, one-half, and three-quarter positions; and finally to the point of coincidence. Likewise, the series could be run in the other direction, from coincidence to exodus, with reports at the three intervening points. Because coincidence is so much more readily observed than is exodus, with which there is typically associated a rather large variability, this direction of change, from coincidence to exodus, was the one more commonly employed.

A preliminary trial of this method with two practiced observers yielded entirely encouraging results and it was decided to formalize the experiment. Figure 6 shows graphically the results for five observers and a sixth curve, which averages the five. On the abscissae of all curves is uniformly marked off the five positions from exodus (E) to coincidence (C), whereas on the ordinates are plotted the $(P_3 - P_2)$ intervals needed to move the rabbit to those positions. Although it is doubtless desirable to have more points on each curve to establish precisely the shape of the function, the average curve seems not to depart too far from

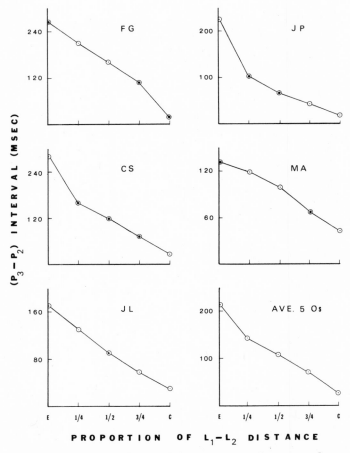

FIGURE 6. Individual fractionation data, together with an average function (lower right). Each point on the individual graphs represents 50 judgments.

linearity. It also has respectable reliability; 1250 settings are represented in these data. At the same time, individual differences in absolute time values may be of some consequence; even in this small population the longest temporal intervals required are about twice as long as the shortest ones. However that may be, the general function seems to say that saltation occurs from some short time just beyond simultaneity of P_2 and P_3, where the threshold of coincidence is found, to an interval of about a quarter of a second, where exodus quells the leaping. Moreover, the time–space tradeoff occurs in a directly proportionate way.

Figure 7 displays the later results of an additional practiced observer, who made judgments of saltation distance for a considerable range of attractant pulse frequencies, pulses representing varying rates of onset and subsidence from 0.5 msec to 16.7 msec from base level to peak. Obviously, the linear character of the relationship is borne out once again. Additionally, the new fact that emerges is that gradient of attack in the attractant appears not to matter at all.

Several variations on the fractionation procedure were introduced, some of which we shall encounter later. One of them should be described at this point, however. Uniformly, throughout the experiment just reported, the spatial direction of leaping was held constant. We have seen that the temporal direction of change, coincidence to exodus or vice versa, was varied, but L_1 was always situated near the wrist and L_2 was located

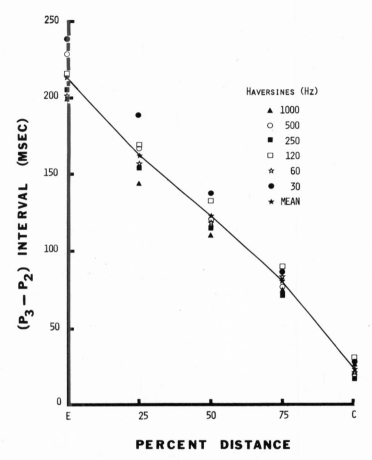

FIGURE 7. Fractionation, by a single observer, when pulses were presented with various onset and subsidence rates, ranging from .5 msec to 16.7 msec (base to peak). Contactors were energized with haversines (versed sine waves) to minimize transients.

10 cm up the arm. Would results be expected to remain the same if the direction of movement were to be reversed? The consequence of such a reversal might have an important bearing on the ultimate explanation of the rabbit's behavior. Sensory nerve impulses, barring artificial and characteristically nonphysiological antidromic ones, run in one direction, always toward the central nervous system. Reversal of the two generating loci "bucks the stream," so to speak. If there should be a difference in saltatory proclivities in the two directions it would at least supply a factor with which to conjure.

The description of the reversal experiment need not detain us long. It was performed with three observers, each making 15 settings apiece at each of the five loci: coincidence, three-quarter, one-half, and one-quarter jumps, and exodus. The values derived were compared with those previously obtained in the 50-trial experiment. There are no significant differences whatever; the rabbit apparently has no relation to the direction of flow of impulses. Indeed, one just concludes the experiment with an enhanced feeling of naivety rather than one of important discovery.

So far there has been no mention of a possible role of stimulus intensity. Typically, all experiments made use of taps presented at a comfortable level and always with the precaution of balancing them for loudness. However, as we shall see, although the temporal disparity between attractant and attractee is the more important determiner of saltation, intensity is not an impotent factor. A minor experiment illustrates the point. At a time when four pulses were being regularly employed (the two terminal markers, P_1 and P_4, and the main saltatory actors, P_2 and P_3), the first and last pulses were intentionally reduced in intensity with a view to "tagging" them, so to speak, to make them readily discriminable from the others. Under these circumstances it was soon found that P_4 was invariably spatially displaced, overshooting the mark by an increment of about 15–20% of the over-all distance. At any rate, the moment the two taps at L_2 (P_3 and P_4) were restored to their 10-dB level, P_4 resumed its normal position at or very near P_3.

Because perturbations of this kind could be created by intensity imbalances it seemed not un-reasonable to assume that the "power of attrac-tion" of the attractant, P_3, might well be related to its intensity. The ($P_3 - P_2$) interval being set at any of a number of different values ranging from 80 to 320 msec, the intensity of P_3 was first brought down to a subthreshold level. Movement of any kind ceased, of course. When intensity was now brought up to threshold leaping was restored, although somewhat tentatively at first and only for the shorter time intervals. However, with fur-ther intensity increase, the leaps were steadily lengthened at all but the longest intervals. Salta-tion is clearly a function not only of temporal dis-parity between the attractant and attractee but of intensity of the attractant as well.

These preliminaries led to a formalization of the experiment, one that paralleled the fractionation procedure already described. The $(P_3 - P_2)$ interval was set, for each observer, at the value empirically established as that for coincidence (in the neighborhood of 20 msec). Intensity was put under the observer's control, and he raised it steadily from a subliminal level to a point yielding a saltatory movement of one of five extents: to exodus, one-quarter, one-half, three-quarters distance, or coincidence. Indeed, he did each of these progressively and then, as a check, repeated the performance in inverse order. Figure 8 shows what happened with two practiced observers. It is clear that, whereas temporal separation sets a fairly rigid limit on the extent of spatial movement possible, the extent of the saltatory leap is also conditioned in a regular and lawful fashion by the intensity of the attractant pulse. For this brief temporal separation, which allows the jump to go the whole distance, the function appears to be approximately a linear one; the extent of the leap is directly proportional to the intensity of the attractant. Just how general this relation is cannot be known until the experiment is repeated with a sufficient N and for sample disparities ranging from that for coincidence to that for exodus.

Some anticipation of what can be expected is provided by an experiment that pits temporal interval against intensity. The question was asked: Would it be possible, with satisfactorily high

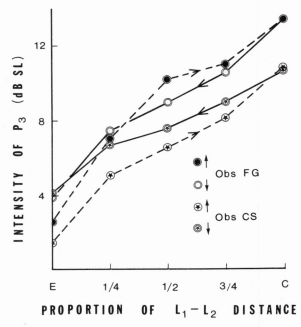

FIGURE 8. Intensity as a factor in determining distance of saltatory leap. Time was uniformly set for the full leap (coincidence).

intensity of P_3 and a setting of the $(P_3 - P_2)$ interval that would bring the leap to the point of coincidence, to alternate the two factors, time and intensity, in such a way as to move the phantom from coincidence to exodus? This "leapfrog" procedure was employed entirely successfully.

The results of these manipulations may be presented, a little unconventionally, as Figure 9. The first move was to reduce intensity progressively from its initial level of 12 dB (sensation level, SL) until the rabbit was jumping only three-quarters the distance toward L_2. For one observer this required an intensive drop to 10.0 dB, for the other to 9.1 dB. Next, leaving the intensities at the new reduced levels, the phantom was moved down to the one-half point by suitable lengthening of the $(P_3 - P_2)$ interval. The new values were 152 and 84 msec, reflecting a characteristic observer difference. Then, holding the interval invariant, intensity was lowered for the second time until a jump of only one-quarter of the L_1-L_2 distance was realized (now 7.1 and 7.5 dB). Finally, saltation was subdued entirely with appropriate lengthening of the time interval (up to 283 and 232 msec, respectively).

What may we say about the relative efficacy of intensity and time in controlling the saltatory leap? It appears that intensity changes can degrade time but cannot improve on it. There is not a simple trading relation between the two variables. We must conclude that temporal interval is the more influential of the two.

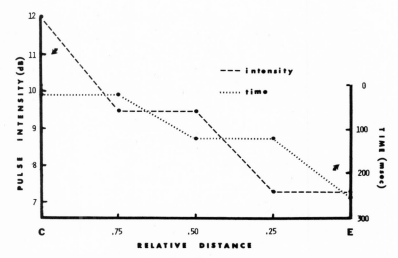

FIGURE 9. The "leapfrog" experiment. Intensity at P_3 and temporal interval between P_2 and P_3 were alternately modified to effect a series of reductions in extent of leaping. The procedure is described in the text. Note that time ($\cdots$) is plotted on the right ordinate, intensity ($---$) on the left.

Incidentally, before the question of the role of intensity is abandoned it should be noted that it is only its influence on the attractant that has been considered. What if P_2, the attractee, were to be strengthened or weakened? Would it become more or less susceptible to influence by the attractant? Would it perhaps resist the drawing power of the final pulse, get "anchored" in place, if its intensity were to be greatly augmented? We have done the experiment, and its conclusion may be stated quite simply. Varying P_2 intensity seems not to matter at all. It makes the P_2 tap noticeably stronger or weaker, of course, but its localization appears not to be affected in any detectable way.

We have now come a considerable distance, seeking understanding of the rabbit's nature, without once raising the important question concerning the essential seat of the process. What must be going on in the cutaneous sensory system to permit such radical deviations from veridicality? The sophisticate in psychophysiology can be counted on to supply an explanation. At least, several have. It is obviously a matter, they say, of rapid spread of shock waves through the skin and of reinforcing and canceling displacements of tissue, in short, of standing waves in the notoriously flexible and yielding human integument. The mechanism is exclusively a peripheral matter. That the shock waves are there in some profusion no one can doubt. It is only necessary to place a sensitive vibration pickup on the skin, amplify, and record its output to find the disturbances.

Likewise, one can bring a single metal plate in close proximity to the skin, letting the tissue itself serve as the second plate of a condenser in a radio frequency circuit, as Rohracher (1949) has done in his Vienna studies, to find that shock waves generated by quite trivial mechanical changes, both on the body surface and inside the body wall, are capable of being transmitted relatively unimpeded over large extents of skin. With all this going on constantly it is scarcely to be wondered at that hypotheses concerning the rabbit's genesis readily assume one or another form of guess about standing, or perhaps reflected, waves. It was our first hunch, and we were glad to have been able to test it before the idea became an obsession.

The test can be a straightforward one. It is only necessary to simulate the conditions used in creating a mechanical rabbit by substituting for the taps brief electrical pulses led directly into the tissue. Whereas this sounds a little spartan, it should be quickly said that very short sinusoidal or square-wave pulses in not too massive dosages can be quite innocuous. Indeed, with suitable precautions with respect to electrodes, loci of stimulation, pulse durations, and some other less crucial variables, electrotactile stimuli may become, in the lower suprathreshold region at least, quite indiscriminable from mechanical pressure pulses.

Three pairs of silver electrodes, each pair separated from the others by isolation transformers, were attached to the forearm with much the same spacing as had obtained in the case of the original

15-tap mechanical rabbit. Trains of five square-wave pulses, each of 2-msec duration, were delivered to the three pairs of electrodes consecutively and without interruption. Clear "taps," brighter in feel than the mechanical ones but otherwise indistinguishable from them, occurred in the predicted places and with the optimal effect in the same parametric range. The essential identity of the two saltatory events is indisputable. Figure 10 demonstrates this with nearly coincident functions for mechanical and electrical stimuli; the small differences depicted lack statistical significance. Because there presumably cannot be surface waves generated by the electrocutaneous pulses, that source of explanation appears to have evaporated.

However, my colleague, Carl Sherrick, who leaves nothing in science to chance except probability theory, has been willing to design and execute a set of painstaking experiments directed at determining just what happens when the skin is disturbed by the impacts of our contactors. His methods were highly sensitive and ingenious; his results were beyond debate.

There are several possible approaches to the difficult and complicated problem of measuring velocities and amplitudes of shock waves through the skin. As a consequence, one gets little comfort from a literature that represents a heterogeneity of methods, types of tissue sampled, and, inevitably, results. The attack in our laboratory was a

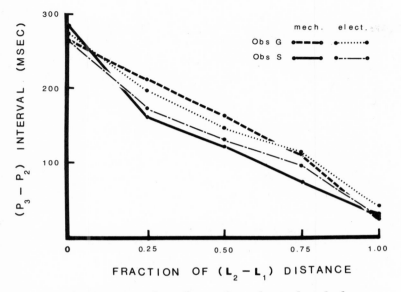

FIGURE 10.   The effects of mechanical and electrical stimuli compared. The differences between the
two lack statistical reliability.

multiple one and involved several kinds of stimulating pulse, both mechanoelectric and photoelectric sensors, a variety of bodily loci to be sampled, and recording techniques ranging from simple oscilloscope records to the stored memory of a signal averager.

The initial step was to replicate what we have come to think of as the "standard" rabbit—five taps on each of three bimorph contactors spaced 10 cm apart. In this instance, however, the middle contactor served as a pickup and the temporal gap between the first and third stimulators was closed. This arrangement reduces to a 20-cm, 10-tap rabbit, of course, with a wave detector midway between L_1 and L_2. With appropriate timing to give well-distributed hopping, the pickup was moved about in a search for local motions. None of any kind was found except near the terminal vibrators and these fell off rapidly as the probe was moved away from them.

A second experiment featured the electrocutaneous rabbit, electrodes being substituted for contactors. There was no detectable movement of tissue at any point tested along the path from L_1 to L_2, including the stimulation sites themselves. Assuming sensitivity of the recording system to have been great enough to reveal their presence, the experiment also negated the possibility that contractile elements, stimulated by the electric current, could be responsible for the creation of minute movements, twitches, or tensions that might generate the false localizations of saltation.

The reduced mechanical rabbit was now substituted for the standard one. Time was adjusted to yield a 50% leap, and the pickup bimorph was positioned at the midpoint of the L_1–L_2 distance. If an enhancement of the displacement wave occurs here it should be discoverable. None was found. It should be said, however, that the very presence of a bimorph, which at best adds an appreciable static pressure (about 2 gm) to the skin, may so load the system as to suppress any tiny displacements that may otherwise exist there. This difficulty was obviated by substituting for the recording bimorph a photoelectric pickup, the Fotronic Sensor. This instrument makes use of fiber optics to deliver a concentrated light patch to the skin and to pick up the reflection from it and conduct the light back to the photoelectric cell. The probe does not touch the skin surface but is simply supported close to it, so that transient changes in reflectance will be mirrored in the electrical response of the cell.

Another possible source of unnecessary complication was also circumvented. The 2-msec rectangular pulses we had ordinarily been using contained, just because they were abrupt square waves, a broad spectrum of energies. Velocity of wave propagation through any medium is a function of frequency, and the waves traveling over and through the skin tissues can be expected to alter their frequency composition, and therefore their form, at various distances from the source. For the rectangular stimulus wave, therefore, there was substituted a wave having a relatively gradual onset and offset (a "haversine"), which could be counted on to scatter relatively little energy throughout the sound spectrum and therefore to simplify velocity calculations.

At the recording end, the output of the Fotronic Sensor was led to a signal averager. Transient stimuli were delivered at L_1, at a rate of one per second for a total of 32 successive presentations, the changes at the Sensor being stored in the memory of the signal averager. When subsequently transferred to an X–Y plotter there was produced a permanent record of the waveform of the displacement throughout its course. The vibratory signal was simultaneously recorded, so that wave velocity and relative displacement amplitude could be analyzed out at various distances from the source of disturbance.

Figure 11 gives a graphic record of the displacement waves at the contactor (lowest trace, where t_s' is the movement into the skin actuated by a 300-Hz haversine) and displacements of the surface of the dorsal forearm at five successive 1-cm steps away from the contactor. The upward deflections, t_1 to t_5, are the first indications of the presence of the wavefront and represent outward displacements of the skin. Downward deflections, corresponding to the important changes in contactor position, those into the tissue, are designated t_1' to t_5'. From these records it is possible to calculate the velocity of wave conduction. For this experiment it is approximately 5.5 m/sec if

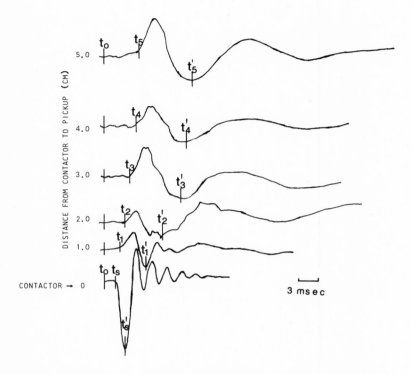

FIGURE 11.   Displacement waves: t_s' = motion of the contactor, activated by a 300-Hz haversine; t_1 to t_5 = outward displacements of the skin of the dorsal forearm at five successive 1-cm steps away from the contactor; t_1' to t_5' = inward displacement of the skin, corresponding to initial direction of contactor motion. Curves traced from an X–Y plotter.

the t' measures are used and 13.3 m/sec if the initial onset, t, is taken as the significant event. One has to decide which index is the right one. Another possible measure is the slope of the waves, which in these records indicates velocity amplitude. Moreover, it is only the surface ripple that is being recorded, of course. Shear waves beneath the epidermis are certainly present, and it is a moot point as to whether deep and surface waves travel at the same speed and are subject to the same mechanical impedances. Because no one has yet seen how to deal with this problem, the two are ordinarily taken to be equivalent or highly correlated. But they may not be.

The figure of 5.5 m/sec (or perhaps 13.3 m/sec) is not a universal one. It was the important one for us, of course, because nearly all quantitative data have been derived from experiments on the dorsal forearm. But measures of wave velocity on soft, relatively flabby tissue and also on more tightly stretched skin lying over a bony substrate have been taken. Samples were obtained on abdomen, shin, and thigh, both ventral and dorsal. Figure 12 shows what changes were brought about when the shin was the "subject." Whether one takes the inward or the outward deflection, speed has increased to 63.5 m/sec, over 11 times the arm velocity, and there is considerably better preservation of stimulus frequency over the same distance. In the softer tissues there is a progressive lowering of the "characteristic frequency" of the displacement wave as it travels.

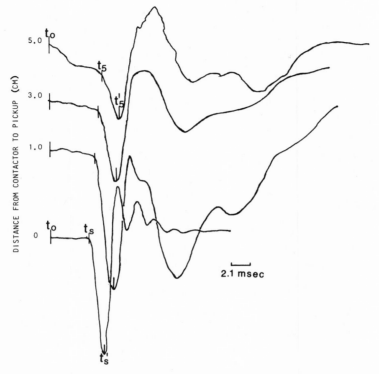

FIGURE 12.   Displacement waves for tissue over-
lying the shin. Wave velocity, calculated at 63.5 m/sec,
is approximately 11 times that on the arm.

71

The crucial question coming out of all this is, of course: Is there anything in the study of traveling waves in the skin that provides a clue as to the underlying cause or causes of saltation? Thus far, all testimony has been in the negative; indeed, everything points to a nonperipheral locus of the saltatory effect. We are presumably dealing with an essentially central seat of the phenomenon; at least, the important occurrences lie downstream of the integument itself. This conclusion is reinforced by some further considerations yet to come.

Now, prior to making a fresh start in a new direction, let us review briefly our state of knowledge about "what makes the rabbit run." We have seen that the phenomenon exists most vividly in the multiple-tap condition but that it can be found with a minimum of two of them, one at each of two loci. The addition of a marker, a single localizing tap, greatly facilitates the quantitative analysis that can be accomplished through a fractionation procedure. The rabbit can go great distances either with or against the flow of afferent nerve impulses; indeed, it can go in more than one direction at once. Time between taps is the great determiner of leaping distance but stimulus intensity is not without influence, too. It can become the controlling variable within the limits set by time. Finally, it is not only mechanical taps that arouse the rabbit to activity; direct electrical stimulation of the skin can act as a surrogate for mechanical pressure. This fact, combined with a fruitless effort to find the necessary motions in the skin, speaks strongly for a central, rather than a peripheral, seat of the phenomenon.

The facts are obviously beginning to add up. If a positive explanation of origin is not at hand as yet, it is perhaps because there are not enough facts or perhaps because those we possess are epiphenomenal or, worse, lacking in pertinence. There is something to be said for varying every known factor, at least in a qualitative way, and attempting to enhance or degrade the basic effect. In an effort to do just this, we have manipulated the attractant not only intensitively but with respect to its very nature. The question came up first when we were doing electrocutaneous experiments. What would be the effect of presenting the initial train of pulses at L_1 electrically and supplying a mechanical rather than an electrical attractant at L_2? We tried it, and it worked; the hops spaced out promptly. The next obvious step was to make the first train mechanical and the attractant electrical. That also worked. We had our first hybrid rabbits!

Since that time several other combinations have been attempted. Two of them are quite spectacular. One involves heat or heat–pain at L_2. This is accomplished quite easily with the aid of a flash cube of the type used in conjunction with Instamatic cameras. If held near the skin at L_2 and masked to allow only a tiny area to be radiated by the flash, and if triggered at the right time in relation to a train of mechanical pulses at L_1, the intense warmth or stabbing heat–pain (if the heat source is placed close to the skin) proves to be an adequate attractant and distributes the hops nicely. The major defect of the method is the havoc it wreaks with research budgets; every trial calls for expending another flash bulb! The other substitute attractant is intense cold. Dr. Roger Cholewiak, of our laboratory, solved this problem, a considerably more difficult one than that at the other end of the thermal scale, by rapidly cooling a 1-cm diameter brass contactor touching the skin at L_2. Figure 13 shows the cold stimulator and its internal arrangements. A nonflammable gas, dispensed by aerosol cans and capable of producing a $-45°C$ freeze, was gated into the tube and against the brass contactor. The time course of the cooling was monitored by an iron–constantan thermocouple. Baseline temperature could be restored by warming the brass contactor with a nichrome wire heater.

In both instances, those in which warm and those in which cold attractants were used, it was possible to distribute multiple mechanical taps at L_1 into the L_1–L_2 space, and it was even possible to experiment with the reduced rabbit. However, no observer succeeded, with either warmth or cold, in fractionating the full distance. With cold, travel extended maximally to 60%; with warmth it was somewhat less, under 50%. However, if pain was aroused the leap could be greater. There are some remarkably natural traits on exhibit here.

One interesting procedural variant involved the "deadening" of the L_2 region by local anesthesia,

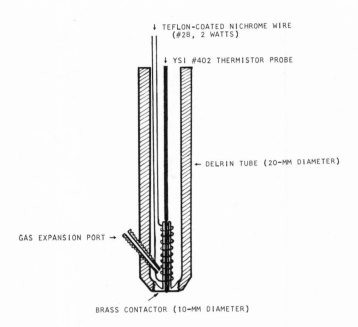

FIGURE 13. Cross section of the stimulator used at L_2 to deliver a "pulse" of cold. Rapidly expanding gas (MS-240, Matheson Scientific Co.) is directed at the brass contactor through a port on the side. The Nichrome wire heater returns the stimulator temperature to baseline when activated by the thermistor probe.

a 2% procaine solution with epinephrine (to confine action of the drug) being driven into the skin electroendosmotically. Stimulation at L_1 consisted of a "locator" pulse followed a second later by a sequence of six taps. A single pulse at L_2 was ineffective until deep receptors were called in with a powerful tap the strength of which was sufficient to cut through the anesthesia and unleash the rabbit. In a second experiment, a rectangular patch of skin 7×4 cm in size, lying between L_1 and L_2 but including neither, was deeply anesthetized. With multiple taps on L_1 and a single one on L_2 the rabbit marched straight through the "dead" area. Observationally, the only difference from the normal rabbit was that the taps felt somewhat deeper and less bright, that is, having less of the "contact" quality about them, but this is true, of course, in any local skin anesthesia. This experiment surprised no one; peripheral alterations that do not produce sensation should not affect the rabbit in any way.

We have had little occasion to consider topographic variations in saltation. Because the rabbit can jump long distances and in different directions, and because any general area of the skin seems to be suitable ground for bringing forth the phenomenon, minute exploration of different cutaneous regions does not, at first blush, appear to be profitable. Actually, a possibly highly important feature of the saltation effect has to do with topographic matters. In trying various placements of contactors on the arm it was somewhat surprising to find that, whereas the rabbit would make quite large leaps with the contactors in the longitudinal orientation, transverse placement often resulted in weak and uncertain taps, even when the distance was quite short. In some locations even separations as small as 5 cm resulted in poor saltation. At very brief $(P_3 - P_2)$ intervals, for example, there might be coincidence or close to it, but lengthening the interval brought about a more or less abrupt reduction to veridical localizations. P_3 remained at L_2 but P_2 seemed to spring back to L_1. No fractionation of the reduced rabbit was possible under such conditions, of course; indeed, it was impossible to observe a phantom at all.

We suspected the basic dermatomal organization of the cutaneous nerves to be responsible, and, to the end that our somewhat hazy hypothesis might be tested, the ventral side of the hand was selected for minute exploration. Four spinal roots arborize into the hand, the sixth, seventh, and eighth cervical, and the first thoracic. It was found that when L_1 and L_2 were both confined to C8 in the palm, good, continuous saltation occurred; but when L_2 was moved out of the area to any of the other three dermatomes, the rabbit ceased to jump. Somewhat similar results were obtained with transverse orientation of contactors on the forearm, although here the distinctions were not as sharp. Indeed, there is less agreement about the dermatomal limits here than in the hand. Placing two contactors on opposite sides of the forearm, front and back, leads only to completely isolated action of the two with a total absence of induced saltation, yet the loci are only 7 inches or less apart circumferentially. Compare this with the extensive leaping over a distance more than double this distance, up the arm from wrist to shoulder.

In the exploratory study of the forearm the opportunity was created for vivid hopping to occur by delivering five successive taps at L_1 and another five at L_2, the interstimulus interval being uniformly 63 msec. The two contactors were positioned on opposite sides of the arm, L_1 ventrally, L_2 dorsally. In successive trials, L_1 was moved progressively on the radial circumference toward L_2, the positions of all ten taps being noted. At whatever level of the arm this was tried, near the elbow or near the wrist, the two contactors stood apart for about two-thirds of the transit. Then, somewhat abruptly, saltatory motion developed at L_2 and spread rapidly until there was uniform hopping around the remaining arc. This experiment calls for difficult manipulations, and we are not satisfied with the efforts to date. It is not easy to apply equal pressures and preserve equivalent intensities at two sites on the skin simultaneously, yet systematically vary position and timing to get the optimal saltatory response. But this experiment, properly performed, could be crucial. The phenomena just described have to be considered along with other related indications, for example, the fact that in the bilateral placement of L_1 and L_2 there is uniformly a failure of the rabbit to jump the midline of the body unless there is also an additional stimulator located there. Instead, there appears to be a distinct "hole" in the pattern where it passes over to the opposite side. This is readily demonstrated on both ventral and dorsal thorax, on the abdomen, and on the forehead. If the taps are strong enough there is some travel on both sides of the line but a typical weakening occurs at the midpoint itself.

We are coming to the belief that we are dealing with a fundamental property of the nervous system and it may have far-reaching implications. Is it a dermatomal boundary that prohibits the saltatory leap? If so, we are in possession of a powerful neurological probe, one that may have practical and clinical value for testing the integrity of the nervous system. Perhaps it has become obvious why our bucolic friend tends to maintain for us, from day to day in our laboratory, a steady state of excitement.

III

Saltation in the Major Senses

In the last chapter we put the rabbit through its paces—or perhaps it would be better to say that we let him frolic through its pages—and discovered that he is all but omnipresent, at least when he is sought in the proper places. You have perhaps come to think of him as a peculiarly and exclusively cutaneous creature. For some time we did, too, despite our careful proofs that the saltatory effect has a central seat. Then the sunlight of reason broke through. If the phenomenon is a cortical or other central event, why should it be necessary for it to be triggered always through somesthetic channels?

The answer proved simple; cutaneous stimulation is not the exclusive precursor. The saltatory effect can be evoked by way of either of the "major" sensory avenues, audition or vision. We found the auditory form first, then the visual, and we shall take them up in that order. The conditions for the production of the two differ considerably, and naturally so. We are dealing with a spatial phenomenon, essentially one of erroneous spatial localization. Vision is our great spatial sense, and the finest spatial discriminations we can make get processed in terms of visual impressions. Indeed, so accurate are we with our visual spatial judgments, so precisely do we judge the coincidence of two contours in space, that a deliberate attempt has been made throughout the history of science to reduce observational readings to those involving the visual juxtaposition of a needle or scale. It certainly seems that vision would be a difficult sense to perturb with respect to spatial affairs. Audition, however, is the channel of choice where temporal distinctions are to be made, whereas it deals with spatial matters only in a secondary and derived way. Helmholtz (1962, p. 173) observed that "the ear is eminently the organ for small intervals of time" and urged, for astronomical purposes, the setting of time coincidences by clicks rather than by light flashes. The auditory system has to be organized pretty much along "dead-beat" lines if it is to follow with fidelity the driving forces impinging on it, if it is to process high-pitched tones or mediate such phenomena as beats and musical consonances and dissonances. The ear approaches spatial tasks with somewhat less than the eye's superb equipment for resolving spatial relations yet does passably well, in many instances, with sound localization by dint of converting spatial cues to temporal ones. On the whole, however, the ear should be easier to deceive than the eye in spatial matters.

A straightforward experiment shows that it is. Seven small loudspeakers, nominally identical,

were equally spaced on an arc which ranged from
45° to the left of the sagittal plane of the body
to 45° to the right (see Figure 14). The matter
of identity of stimuli needs to be stressed; there
should be no local cues that might serve to identify a particular speaker or to cause it to be differ-
entiated from its fellows on the basis of anything
other than its location in space. Minimizing of
cues is not readily accomplished. In this experiment it was necessary to filter the speakers with
a narrow bandpass network to achieve sufficient
similarity of click pitch even though the instruments shared common manufacture. Although the
room in which the study was carried out was not
strictly anechoic, cloth curtains were hung appro-
priately to minimize reflections, and prolonged
reverberations, which could easily vitiate any such
experiment, clearly did not occur.

Presentation of the stimulus clicks was by a
combination of Tektronix pulse generator, initiating 100-μsec square waves that were then ampli-
fied and attenuated, and a Tally tape reader, seven
channels of which determined rate, trial interval,
pattern pair interval, and intertrial report period.
Interstimulus intervals ranged between 25 and 80
msec in four steps. All clicks were equated for
loudness before a session was begun with any particular observer.

The task set was to discriminate a pattern having a succession of seven clicks passing from left
to right, one on each speaker, from a sequence
involving only three speakers spread over the

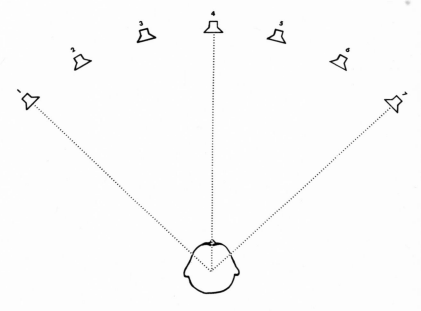

FIGURE 14. Arrangement of the seven identical
loudspeakers in the auditory "confusion" experiment.

same distance: No. 1, No. 4, and No. 7. Although various combinations were tried, the really impressive confusion arose when the 1–7 sequence was either preceded or followed by two clicks on No. 1, three clicks on No. 4, and two clicks on No. 7. Speakers 2, 3, 5, and 6 were, of course, silent in this instance. It must be assumed that, if an observer cannot tell the difference between these two click progressions, a genuine saltatory effect must be occurring in auditory space. The results obtained from 14 observers in this experiment testify that it does indeed occur.

In other trials the same observers were presented single patterns, some involving true 1–7 progressions and some containing one or another concentration of clicks (e.g., three on No. 1, three on No. 4, one on No. 7; or, five on No. 1, one on No. 4, one on No. 7). In general, the more evenly spread out the clicks were the poorer was the discrimination between it and the regular order; the more the clicks were centered on one source the more readily could the observer distinguish it from a standard 1–7 pattern. Such a result surely is not unexpected.

This experiment greatly resembles one performed independently by Jenkins and his students at the University of Minnesota and which was reported by them at the Boston meeting of the Psychonomic Society in the fall of 1974 (Bremer, Pittenger, & Jenkins, 1974, p. 244). Stimulated by our report of the cutaneous rabbit, they looked for an auditory analog and devised a situation in which three loudspeakers, hidden behind a curtain in front of the observer, emitted trains of clicks, some regularly spaced and some irregular. The middle speaker fell in the sagittal plane; the others were placed at equal distance at either side. Three clicks were introduced in each speaker, and the interclick interval was varied from short to long (10–250 msec). When times were either very long or irregular, localization was quite accurate; when of moderate duration, there was some spreading of the trains from their true location; but when interstimulus intervals were short, the spreading went so far as to give the impression of a uniform linear distribution. Obviously, the parallel with the cutaneous rabbit is quite exact and their findings fit what we know of auditory saltation.

Creation of the auditory saltatory illusion emboldened my colleague, Carl Sherrick, to ask whether auditory space might not be a suitable medium for fractionation, in the style of the reduced rabbit of the cutaneous experiments. Accordingly, he set up a pair of booms in the sound room, each bearing on its end an earphone of good quality. The two phones, equidistant from the middle of the observer's head, could be accurately adjusted both with respect to each other and with respect to the interaural axis. The head was securely held in a harness to prevent movement; a dim fixation light also kept the eyes from moving. Two arrangements, sampling different portions of auditory space, entered the experimental design. The two are shown in Figure 15. The L_1–L_2 arc subtends 40° in the left anterior quadrant;

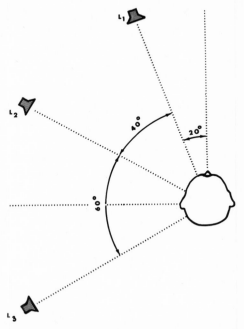

FIGURE 15. The fields in two auditory fractionation experiments. In one, the arc subtended is 40° in
the left anterior quadrant; in the other, the field cov-
ered occupies the middle 60° opposite the left ear.

L_2–L_3 is lateralized to the left and covers a 60° arc.

Clicks from the two phones were picked up by a microphone and were sent to a General Radio sound and vibration analyzer to insure both constant frequency composition and freedom from contamination by adventitious reflections, etc. Phone L_1 (L_2 in the instance of the lateral 60° arc) delivered P_1 and P_2; Phone L_2 (L_3) provided P_3. At the beginning of a session there was obtained, for each observer, the absolute threshold to P_1 (P_2 is physically identical with it), and intensity was arbitrarily set at 40 dB SL. P_3 was matched in loudness to P_1 by the observer. All clicks were initiated by Tektronix waveform and pulse generators. As with the cutaneous reduced rabbit, P_1 preceded P_2 by 800 msec; there was then a variable silent interval (0–600 msec) under the control of the observer and then P_3 was produced at the second locus.

In all, eight observers served in the experiment, most of them doing the distance fractionation for both auditory fields in a large number of repetitions, sometimes starting at coincidence and moving through the three quartile points to exodus and sometimes progressing in the reverse direction.

There are somewhat large individual differences, but there can be no doubting the trend. Observationally, P_2 travels smoothly and easily from one end of the arc to the other, its apparent position always being determined by the time interval between the second and third clicks. There appeared to be no significant difference between time settings for the two segments of the auditory field under test, and the results of the total of 290 observations are therefore combined in a single graph (see Figure 16).

Far less attention has been given by us to the auditory rabbit than to either the tactual or visual ones. There are therefore many questions, chiefly prompted by analogous saltatory behavior in somesthesis, that must remain unanswered for the time being. We simply have not done the work required to get the answers, although it is certain that there are answers to be had.

We turn now to vision, the modality on which we are most dependent to inform us of the location of objects in space. The first search was conducted with the aid of light-emitting diodes, or LEDs, these having been selected for their prompt onset and offset, certainly not for the amount of light they emit. The temporal pattern of the reduced rabbit was reproduced by a Tally tape reader, and an interflash interval in the neighborhood of 100 msec was tried. With two amber LEDs about 5° apart and with fixation off to the side about 25–30° from the flashing fields, the saltatory effect was displayed clearly, jumps of about one-quarter of the L_1–L_2 distance being reported almost immediately by several observers familiar with the cutaneous analog.

It was not expected that spatially and temporally separated light flashes falling at or near the fovea would surprise us with saltatory antics, and

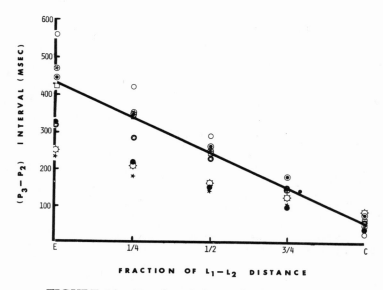

FIGURE 16. Results of the auditory fractionation experiment. Each symbol is a different observer. The line is drawn through median values for the eight observers.

they did not. However, why so far into the visual periphery? Observation is generally both difficult and unreliable there. The situation with the visual rabbit is much the same as that in scotopic observation. The French astronomer, Arago, is responsible for the near paradox: "In order to perceive a very dimly lit object, it is necessary not to look at it" (von Helmholtz, 1924–1925, Vol. II, p. 332). The rule is the same for rabbits, whether dimly or brightly lit. To see our kind of rabbit you must not stare directly at it but instead let its procreators, the two light flashes, fall well into indirect vision. The relatively loose organization of the peripheral retina appears to be the necessary milieu for genesis. That is presumably why the effect has not been discovered long ago. Why should anyone, in designing a visual experiment, intentionally put two separated light spots into a sector of the visual field calling for the greatest observational inconvenience, not to say stress, and then further disjoin them in time and, moreover, at intervals uncongenial to the production of normal synthetic movement? As we shall see, however, in visual saltation great liberties may be taken with space, time, and even intensity and wavelength without destroying the basic effect. Indeed, considering that we are dealing with a prime instance of perceptual metastability, we have here a remarkably stable phenomenon.

Just how far into the periphery it is necessary to go to produce minimally perceptible saltation has not been determined with any precision. A careful psychophysical experiment entailing a statistically adequate number of readings and observers would be required to get the answer, and we have not done it. Moreover, one would have to optimize all other variables, and we are as yet not that knowledgeable about the variables that matter. Meanwhile, it seems almost certain that the rabbit never invades the central macula. We have, however, obtained an occasional clear separation of the phantom from L_1 within $10°$ of the fovea.

Another certainty about the variable of locus is that the extent of leaping is a function of angular subtense from the fovea, at least up to the point where anything like reliable readings can be had. The fractionation experiment was a natural one to attempt, and three important decisions concerning its conduct were made at the outset. The first was that considerably higher intensities would have to be made available. This was accomplished through the use of the General Radio Strobotac and its ancillary Stroboslave, both capable of delivering several million beam candles. Their output was conducted from outside the darkroom by Crofon light guides, which terminated in tiny light boxes equipped with crossed Polaroid filters and ground glass viewing screens that subtended 40 min of arc at the eye. A second change involved the adoption of somewhat finer gradations in the scale of judged distances than had obtained in the cutaneous experiments. In a preliminary exploration, judgments of 10% distance steps proved to be feasible. The third decision was

that all major meridians of the visual field would
be sampled and at a sufficient number of points
to yield adequate coverage of the total useful visual field. Figure 17 displays a retinal map on
which are indicated all retinal points tested. Visual
angles ranged from 15° to 40° in 5° steps. Note,
in passing, that there are no fixations recorded on
the vertical meridian, and those recalling what
happened at the body's midline in somesthesis can
guess why. In any case, we shall return to this
matter in another context later.

Beginning either with exodus, which characteristically required about the same temporal separation of P_2 and P_3 as had obtained in the cutaneous
experiments, or with flash simultaneity, the observer moved progressively in steps of 10% of the
overall distance between light patches by adjust-
ing the interflash interval. It is to be observed that
the end of the time scale at which L_1 and L_2 were
illuminated simultaneously is not being referred
to, as it was in touch, as the point of "coincidence." Although there has been an assiduous
search for the conditions that can lead to the full
jump to coincidence with the attractant, this apparently does not occur in visual saltation. Perhaps
this is evidence of the relative stability of vision
as compared with touch; perhaps it is only an indi-
cation that we have not looked in the right places
for the phenomenon. Whatever the answer, the
longest leaps appear to be no greater than 80% of
the distance, and these occur with some rarity.

The remaining important details of the experiment may be summarized quickly, for some of

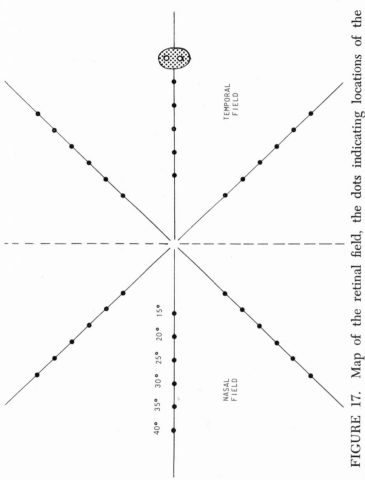

FIGURE 17. Map of the retinal field, the dots indicating locations of the flashing light spots. All major radii were tested (except the vertical; see text) at visual angles of 15, 20, 25, 30, 35, and 40°. The light spots, together with their common surround, are represented at the 40° temporal position.

them parallel those of the cutaneous fractionation work. Timing, for example, was carried out by a system of Tektronix waveform and pulse generators, adequate spacing of trials being given to obviate afterimagery or light adaptation in the test fields. The stimulus lights themselves subtended 0.5° each and were (somewhat arbitrarily) positioned 5° apart. They had a continuous surround, roughly $10 \times 4°$ in size, which was illuminated through fluorescence, an ultraviolet source above and behind the observer's head flooding the surround with "black light." The reason for the existence of a surround becomes apparent when you are reminded of the deleterious effects of the autokinetic phenomenon, discussed in Chapter I.

The average results for three observers, for all 36 fixation positions and the 6 steps of retinal eccentricity tested, are displayed in Figure 18. The first obvious generalization is that very much the same relation holds here as was encountered in somesthesis: the shorter the interflash interval, the greater the saltatory leap. The function here departs from linearity, and it is yet a moot point whether this results from the finer sampling of distances in the visual case or whether there is a real intermodal difference—linear for touch, curvilinear for vision. Much more work obviously must be done on both before this point can be settled. Indeed, there are some statistical matters here that are not going to be settled with observer populations of five and three!

A second clear generalization from the fractionation results has to do with retinal eccentricity.

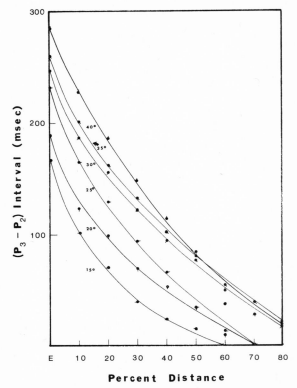

FIGURE 18. Average curves for three observers participating in the visual fractionation experiment.

96

This, of course, was anticipated. Had something like this not been foreseen the visual rabbit might never have been found at all. And although the dependence of magnitude of saltatory leap on degree of excursion into the periphery is clearly shown in the results already displayed, a replotting of the data with interflash interval as the parameter brings the relation out strongly (see Figure 19).

In the fractionation experiment the phenomenal appearance of the stimulus field speaks strongly for a fundamental difference between the two channels, vision and touch, in their mode of functioning. Typically, in touch, when the time interval between P_2 and P_3 is very short and the phantom is either coincident with the attractant or lies very close to it, there is no remnant of P_2 in its "true" position, at L_1. (Occasionally, it must be said, there is; one gets the impression of three taps coexisting, but this is rare and quite unreproducible). In vision, however, such is its mode of operation with respect to "persistence" that at short interstimulus intervals there invariably are seen three stimulus patches simultaneously, the "true" ones at L_1 and L_2 and the phantom, lying somewhere in between. Indeed, at high intensities this appearance lasts for fully 100 msec or more and at lower brightnesses only a little less. This is not to say that precedence judgments could not be made with complete reliability had they been called for, but observers had no real difficulty at any interval duration, up to that for exodus itself,

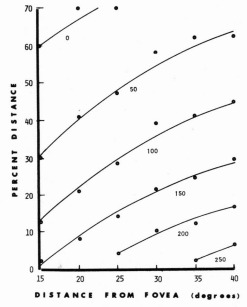

FIGURE 19. A replotting of the data of Figure 18 with interflash interval as the parameter.

retaining a "correct" impression of where L_1 was situated and thus making ready judgments of leaping distance.

Another major difference between touch and vision has to do with the orientation of the receptor organ with respect to the anticipated display. Our use of a fixation light guarantees that orientation, of course. Indeed, there is no real need for the locator pulse, P_1, in the visual instance of the reduced rabbit; it may be eliminated entirely, further simplifying the conditions to what may now be called the "utterly reduced" rabbit. In the fractionation experiment just described, the locator, P_1, was retained simply to make the experiment in the two modalities as comparable as possible. Actually, such retention does neither harm nor good, so far as can be seen, for P_1 is separated from P_2 by a full 800 msec and therefore produces no intraserial effects in the chain of stimulus events. In many subsequent visual experiments it has been dropped as unnecessary baggage.

The next influence to come under scrutiny was that of adaptation. Special steps were taken to insure that observation would always begin under a standard set of conditions. As in the classical experiments on dark adaptation, such as those by Selig Hecht and his students (Hecht & Shlaer, 1938), a fixed period of light adaptation under an illumination intensity approximating that of the laboratory outside the darkroom (about 100 foot-lamberts) preceded all saltation observations. Steps to render absolutely constant dark-adapting conditions were considered to be urgent, for it almost invariably turned out that leaping distances for a given set of stimulating conditions were greater at the beginning of an observation period than a little later, and it was supposed that uncontrolled adaptation might well be responsible.

It would be satisfying to be able to tell you that the role of light and dark adaptation in visual saltation has, at this point, been clearly revealed. Unhappily, such is not the case. It seems to be true that saltatory jumps are greater when a sequence of observations is approached with the light-adapted eye, and that the beginnings of dark adaptation, more frequently than not, are accompanied by a marked reduction in magnitude of the leap. It is also true that, more often than not, prolonged exposure to a relatively dimly lit field, which must be associated with a considerable amount of dark adaptation, tends to allow a return of the relatively longer leaps characteristic of light adaptation. The ultimate revelation of the relation between saltation and adaptation, if there is to be one, will come only after more work has been done on the problem—much more.

Meanwhile, one phenomenon coming out of the adaptation experiments done to date is worth reporting, for it may just be central to some of the rabbit's behavior. If there is given a preliminary 3-min period of light adaptation in which the entire retina is bathed in white light at 100 foot-lamberts and then if saltatory judgments are taken on a regular schedule (simultaneous 2-msec

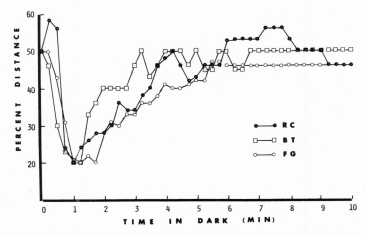

FIGURE 20. Individual curves showing a uniform "dip" in distance of saltatory leap during the first minute of observation in very low illumination ("dark," for all practical purposes).

flashes in the two stimulus fields 30° out in the periphery, the repetitive reduced rabbit sequence of 6-sec duration, flash intensity of about 0.1 foot-lambert, and a 20° surround of roughly one-tenth that luminance), an interesting trend develops. If observation is continuous for from 5 to 30 min, judged leaping distance is found initially to be at or near the 50% point. Soon, within a minute usually, there is an abrupt shortening of the jump to a level of 10–30% of the overall distance; then this is followed by a more or less steady climb back to the midpoint again. All observers showed this remarkable dip and all on about the same time schedule. Figure 20 shows averages of three observers for whom there are the most adequate data. They cover the first 10 min of uninterrupted observation. Figure 21 presents the average readings of 14 different sessions, the data of the same three observers being combined. The mysterious dip seems to be a fixture and it is not readily explained away in terms of the influence of adaptation, whether differential as between rods and cones or exclusively by one or the other.

Actually, the curves in Figure 20 represent an oversimplification. If one stops to think about what must happen when lights at L_1 and L_2 are presented absolutely simultaneously it should be realized that the designation of one of them as the attractant and the other as the attractee is necessarily spurious. The two light flashes were equal in every respect; they were triggered by the same pulse generator and were not only simultaneous in onset and offset but were in phase with

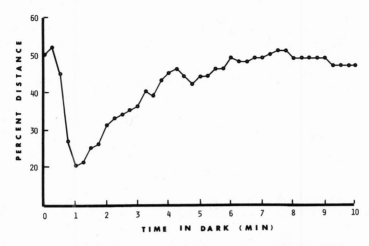

FIGURE 21. Average curve for data displayed in Figure 20.

one another. It follows that each should be both attractant and attractee. Except in the 50% region, where, so to speak, a second-order coincidence ought to occur, there should be two phantoms, one attracted by L_2, the other by L_1. There are. Indeed, because all stimulus influences are balanced, the graph of Figure 21 should contain a second curve, the mirror image of the first. Empirically, this is what happens, at least in some instances and with some observers when they are instructed to direct attention in quick succession to both the upper and the lower portions of the interstimulus space. (It should be recalled that the two light patches are disposed vertically to keep them equidistant from the fixation point.) Attending to both takes some doing and makes for lively observation and report, but witness an instance in Figure 22. This represents five continuous minutes of judging the locations of two complementary rabbits induced 30° in the periphery after a 3-min preadaptation period. There is general agreement among observers that the upper phantom is dimmer than the lower one, and this is as inexplicable as the dip itself.

In an effort to get at the underlying cause or causes of the dip, a manipulation was undertaken in which fixation was systematically shifted through small arcs at fixed time intervals. Thus, at the conclusion of the regular 3-min light adaptation period, fixation was initially held for 5 min at a position 5° above the horizontal meridian at 20° nasally. Continuous reports of leaping distance were made. Then, on signal at the end of 5 min,

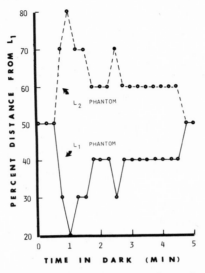

FIGURE 22. Dual phantoms elicited when the $(P_3 - P_2)$ interval is zero.

fixation was shifted downward by 5° and again held for 5 min. The sequence then involved going down 5° below that, then back to the fixation lamp on the horizontal meridian, and finally back to the original fixation point again. The total 25-min session therefore provided five "fresh" peripheral regions for the test flashes.

All observers obtained postfixational dips of the kind with which we are now familiar at all fixation stations, and all experienced double phantoms, as expected. The hypothesis then suggested itself that simply moving the eyes might be sufficient to create the dip. This was tried many times, always with a return to the fixation point just used and always with the same results, completely negative ones. Finally, at the 5-min mark, eyes were closed; they were reopened at the end of a minute and the original fixation point was regained. This maneuver proved useless, also. Apparently, the dip is associated with stimulation of a "fresh," i.e., new and different, retinal area, even though that area may be all but contiguous with the one previously excited. Presumably, we ought to be translating the fixations and retinal areas into patches of the occipital cortex but it is doubtful that our understanding of the phenomenon would thereby be greatly enhanced.

With our attention so much on adaptation and related processes usually considered to have their seat in the retina, it may be well for us to remind ourselves of the important fact that we are dealing with a phenomenon that, at least in its somesthetic incarnation, has pretty well proved to be central

in origin. Can there be adduced any evidence in
the visual sphere that either confirms or contra-
dicts this belief? Yes, fortunately we are equipped
with two eyes which, at any given moment, may
be stimulated differentially; also, they are known
to be connected to the brain in a most orderly,
if somewhat complicated, fashion. Obstructions
can be set up in the optical path from the stimulus
fields to the eyes such that the light flash from
L_1 falls on one retina and that from L_2 at a noncor-
responding point on the other. The experiment
was duly performed, with the not unexpected result that a stable phantom appeared promptly in
the region of the 50% mark. Unless one wishes to
assume that some most remarkable efferent events
have been triggered by this manipulation, the conclusion seems inescapable that the visual rabbit
also has his home in the brain. Indeed, this proof
is so direct as to constitute the best we have of
the central seat of the saltation effect.

The visual field being organized so nicely along
geometrical lines and the visual stimulus having
so many dimensions with which to work, it is possible to "tag" our light flashes in a number of
ways, and this permits experiments that cannot
be carried out in other sense channels. There is,
for example, the matter of color. The flash at L_1
can be given one hue and that at L_2 a discrimin-
ably different one. When light spots are being pro-
jected well out into the periphery, as ours are, this
is not an easy thing to arrange. The relative color-
lessness of the spectrum that far out in the peripheral retina is well known. High intensities are

needed if color is to be retained, especially in small fields. However, it was possible to make one light spot yellow and the other blue with roughly balancing filters. In macular viewing the two were approximately equally bright. Then, removed 30° into the temporal periphery, the two fields were flashed synchronously and a double phantom appeared immediately, the one nearest the blue field being blue and that nearest the yellow field, yellow. There was some temporary instability; then the two phantoms became locked together at the 50% position and we now had a white rabbit from the yellow and blue procreators. In similar fashion, a green light at one spot combined with a red one at the other to give us a yellow rabbit. What this says for the locus of the color-mixing process is not immediately clear, but the facts are likely to be of interest to those concerned with color theory. We have long known, of course, that brain color mixtures can be created binocularly but this is surely a new route to the brain in color research.

When we were considering the cutaneous rabbit the question was raised as to what would happen if we made the attractant ambiguous, and we saw that if the initiating pulse, P_2, is followed by two simultaneous attractants lying in either direction from L_1, there are generated two rabbits. The same experiment can be done in vision. With the aid of a totally reflecting prism it was arranged for L_2 to appear both above and below L_1, so that when L_2 was illuminated it would occupy two locations equidistant from L_1. With a zero time difference between the two flashes at L_1 and L_2 (and the additional image of L_2) there were now created two phantoms and these, added to the already existing three lights, contributed to a total of five approximately evenly spread out flashes. Figure 23 shows how the fields were arranged.

As you will be able to conclude by now, quite a few of the visual experiments to date are no more than exploratory and quite qualitative in character. When it is considered that so little time has transpired since the first observation of visual saltation, a remarkable number of bypaths have opened up and many of them beckon enticingly. Moreover, there are major variables that have so far remained quite neglected. What of flash duration: is it important? Whereas most experiments have been carried out with flashes of the order of 2–5 msec, a preliminary set of trials with 100-msec exposures has not destroyed the rabbit. Apparently, duration is not critical. What of size or angular subtense at the retina? Next to nothing has been done on this, although it is known that viewing the field through a magnifier of about $4\times$ does not disrupt the saltatory process.

Recently, a major alteration has been made in the apparatus to permit much higher intensities of flash and to provide, through the use of fluorescent lamps, for relatively long, steady exposures. The shape of the fields has also been altered, horizontal slits yielding the same light flux replacing the original circular patches. It has been found

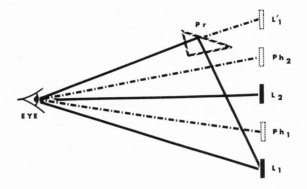

FIGURE 23. The optical paths involved in dupli-
cating the L_1 image. As in touch, phantoms are generated between L_2 and both L_1 and L_1'.

that more satisfactory distance judgments can be
made with the elongated fields. Preliminary experiments with the new light sources tell us a little
about the role of intensity. It should be recalled
that, in the somesthetic instance, intensity has
proved to be not unimportant but less prepotent
than time in controling the saltatory leap. Intensity was not made a variable at the beginning of
work on the visual effect. Rough, almost cursory
exploration of the role of intensity led to the con-
viction that dim lights hopped better than bright
ones and, largely for that reason, quite low luminance levels, in both attractant and attractee, were
used throughout the early visual experiments. Indeed, because low intensities are far more comfortable to live with during prolonged observation
periods in the darkroom, generally low luminances
have been selected throughout the visual work
described thus far. However, although there has
been no systematic experiment involving statistically adequate numbers of readings, there are
scattered observations clearly indicating absolute
intensity level to be of little consequence in gov-
erning the extent of the saltatory leap. More recently, luminances have been made to vary over
a range of better than three log units, the highest
being in the neighborhood of 1000 foot-lamberts,
and what has come to be regarded as the typical
course for simultaneous flashes has, without excep-
tion, been realized, viz., an initial 50% leap, an
early decline (the "dip"), and a gradual return

to the halfway mark. There has not been a visual repetition of the cutaneous "leap-frog" experiment, however, and this needs to be done.

Earlier, when the role of retinal locus in controlling saltation was being described, it was noted that fixation points situated on the vertical meridian were of no avail because L_1 and L_2 necessarily fell on either side of it and the phantom could not contend with the midline barrier. This has been a consistent finding. Taken together with the analogous failure of the cutaneous rabbit to jump the midline of the body, there would seem to be here a phenomenon of more than passing neurological interest. Something more than the bare fact of midline interruption will need to be known, of course, before the full significance of this phenomenon will be in our possession. Are there ways of overcoming the midline gap? Why should there be some kind of continuity on either side of the midline if the barrier cannot be hurdled? What possible roles do such factors as intensity, pulse duration, and the spatial properties of the stimulus play? It is easier to ask the questions than to answer them.

While we are asking questions—and by way of concluding our journey through the saltatory realm—let us scan quickly the unresolved problems with which we are left. In the cutaneous sphere, it would be of interest and possibly of importance to find out what liberties can be taken with pulse timing. How irregular may pulsing be and the forward movement of the phantom be retained? We know the phenomenon must break down at some point along the continuum. Also, there is the interesting matter of preconditioning. It was found, almost accidentally, that repeated "swooping," rapid repetitions of a multitap rabbit, would either facilitate or inhibit the length of the saltatory jumps, depending on the direction in which preliminary movement was induced. This preparatory "tuning" effect could be quite central to the eventual interpretation of the entire phenomenon.

In audition, as has been seen, many things have been neglected to date. There has been little manipulation of even the most fundamental variables. What roles do frequency, intensity, waveform, and duration play? It would be difficult to get much more "basic" than this. There is also a wide range of possibilities with respect to attractant–attractee relationships. In this regard, what differences would be made by variations in frequency and frequency composition (timbre), noise versus tones, or intensity changes? The surface has hardly been scratched.

In vision, are there spatial limits not encountered as yet? Size changes have been mentioned, but there has been no systematic variation of either size or shape. Are there limits to the retinal distances over which the effect can be adduced? We know there are limits of direction and locus. There is a characteristic alteration of phenomenal distance, of which we have not spoken, as test fields are moved further into the periphery. What happens is that there is an augmentation of apparent angular subtense as vision gets more eccentric. This is not a new phenomenon. Writing in the appendix to Helmholtz's great *Physiological optics* (1924–1925) von Kries suggested hanging "a small balance pan by a cord about 2 metres long so as to swing slowly like a pendulum; and place a lighted candle on it. Now observe these vibrations very indirectly at first, and then turn the eyes to look straight at them; it will be astonishing to see how much smaller the motion is when it is perceived more exactly by foveal vision than it appeared to be in indirect vision" (Vol. III, pp. 275–276). What bearing does this phenomenon have on the magnitude of the saltatory leap?

Perhaps the greatest mystery with the visual rabbit is that surrounding what has been referred to as the "dip," the abrupt reduction in jumping distance occurring, apparently quite automatically, after about a minute's observation in semi-darkness. Ways of altering it must be found if it is to be explained. It still seems to be connected with adaptation, but how? One thing that needs to be done is to invest in some longer adaptation periods in the dark before saltation observations are begun. Rods and cones adapt differentially, both to light and darkness. The relative roles of these two sets of receptors in mediating the saltatory response may become clear through control of adaptation.

An experiment still in the planning stage is one in which the retinal area lying between L_1 and L_2 is treated differentially. The idea is to induce local light adaptation in this region, one sufficiently prolonged and intense to "brand" a lasting afterimage there, and to then determine whether such an altered state will influence the rabbit in any way. It should be recalled that local skin anesthesia is not a deterrent to hopping, and the two cases are at least roughly analogous.

Another visual problem has to do with the failure of the leap to go the full distance. Why does the visual phantom not extend to coincidence? Cutaneous and auditory displacements do. Is it possible that the double phantoms, showing up under a restricted set of circumstances in vision but not in the other modalities, bring about a stabilization not found in touch and hearing?

A question that seems to have been answered for somesthesis but not for either audition or vision concerns the matter of the optimal number of pulses that may be processed at one locus without destroying the phantom. What is the number of repetitions that will be tolerated before the impression gets "anchored," so to speak, at one place and fails to leap to another? Something of the order of 15 or so still permits tactile saltation, whereas 20 do not. What are the corresponding numbers for clicks and light flashes?

Finally, just as it is important to know, in touch, what degree of jitter will be tolerated while preserving the phantom, a similar question may be asked for audition and vision. To what extent is it possible to deviate from strict pulse regularity? How deleterious are brief gaps?

We have been asking a lot of questions, more, I fear, than are likely to be answered satisfactorily in the immediate future. Asking questions seems to be inevitable when you have fallen into a rabbit hole. You will recall that Alice Liddell asked herself endlessly, as she was falling down hers, "Do cats eat bats?" but sometimes "Do bats eat cats?" And Lewis Carroll concluded, "as she couldn't answer either question, it didn't much matter how she put it." We think some of our questions at least have answers, and we are confidently looking for the right ones.

References

Benussi, V. Versuche zur Analyse taktil-erweckter Scheinbewegungen. *Archiv für die gesamte Psychologie,* 1916, **36,** 59–135.

Boring, E. G. *Sensation and perception in the history of experimental psychology.* New York: Appleton-Century, 1942.

Bremer, C. D., Pittenger, J. B., & Jenkins, J. J. An auditory illusion similar to the cutaneous "rabbit." *Bulletin of the Psychonomic Society,* October, 1974.

Burtt, H. E. Tactual illusions of movement. *Journal of Experimental Psychology,* 1917, **2,** 371–385.

Donders, F. C. *Anomalies of accommodation and refraction of the eye.* London: New Sydenham Society, 1864.

Gelb, T. Versuche im Gebiete der Raum- und Zeitanschauung. *Berichte über den VI Kongress für experimentelle Psychologie in Göttingen,* Leipzig, 1914, 36–42.

Geldard, F. A., & Sherrick, C. E. The cutaneous "rabbit": a perceptual illusion. *Science,* 1972, **178,** 178–179.

Hecht, S., & Shlaer, S. An adaptometer for measuring human dark adaptation. *Journal of the Optical Society of America,* 1938, **28,** 269–275.

Helson, H., & King, S. M. The *tau* effect: an example of psychological relativity. *Journal of Experimental Psychology*, 1931, 14, 202–217.

Julesz, B. *Foundations of cyclopean perception.* Chicago: University of Chicago Press, 1971.

Licklider, J. C. R., & Miller, G. A. The perception of speech. In S. S. Stevens (Ed.), *Handbook of experimental psychology.* New York: Wiley, 1951. Pp. 1040–1074.

Moncrieff, R. W. Olfactory adaptation and odour likeness. *Journal of Physiology (London)*, 1956, 133, 301–316.

McComas, H. C. *Ghosts I have talked with.* Baltimore: Williams and Wilkins, 1935.

MacKay, D. M. Interactive processes in visual perception. In W. A. Rosenblith (Ed.), *Sensory communication.* New York: Wiley, 1961. Pp. 339–355.

Rohracher, H. *Mechanische Mikroschwingungen des menschlichen Körpers.* Vienna: Urban and Schwarzenberg, 1949.

Sherrick, C. E. Studies of apparent tactual movement. In D. R. Kenshalo (Ed.), *The skin senses.* Springfield, Illinois: Charles C Thomas, 1967. Pp. 331–344.

von Békésy, G. Synchrony between nervous discharges and periodic stimuli in hearing and on the skin. *Annals of Otology, Rhinology, & Laryngology,* 1962, 71, 678–693.

von Békésy, G. *Sensory inhibition.* Princeton: Princeton University Press, 1967.

von Helmholtz, H. L. F. *Treatise on physiological optics.* Rochester: Optical Society of America, 1924–1925. 3 vols.

von Helmholtz, H. L. F. *On the sensations of tone.* New York: Dover, 1962.

Author's Publications

1. The measurement of retinal fatigue to achromatic stimulation. I. *Journal of General Psychology,* 1928, **1**, 123–135.
2. The measurement of retinal fatigue to achromatic stimulation. II. *Journal of General Psychology,* 1928, **1**, 578–590.
3. (with W. B. Crockett) The binocular acuity relation as a function of age. *Journal of Genetic Psychology,* 1930, **37**, 139–145.
4. Brightness contrast and Heymans' law. *Journal of General Psychology,* 1931, **5**, 191–206.
5. (with R. C. Davis) An oscillator and synchronous motor for obtaining exact variable speeds. *Science,* 1931, **73**, 369–370.
6. Foveal sensitivity as influenced by peripheral stimulation. *Journal of General Psychology,* 1932, **7**, 185–189.
7. The description of a case of total color blindness. *Journal of the Optical Society of America,* 1933, **23**, 256–260.
8. The description of a case of total color blindness. *Psychological Bulletin,* 1933, **30**, 609.
9. Flicker relations within the fovea. *Journal of the Optical Society of America,* 1934, **24**, 299–302.
10. The present status of the laws of learning. *University of Virginia Record,* 1934, **22**, 1–7.

11. (with B. von H. Gilmer) A method for investigating the sensitivity of the skin to mechanical vibration. *Journal of General Psychology*, 1934, **11**, 301–310.
12. Is vibratory sensitivity mediated by the "pressure sense"? *Psychological Bulletin*, 1936, **33**, 776.
13. Proceedings of the thirty-second annual meeting of the Southern Society for Philosophy and Psychology. *Psychological Bulletin*, 1937, **34**, 568–572.
14. Proceedings of the thirty-third annual meeting of the Southern Society for Philosophy and Psychology. *Psychological Bulletin*, 1938, **35**, 487–518.
15. "Explanatory principles" in psychology. *Psychological Review*, 1939, **46**, 411–424.
16. The vibratory response of the skin and its relation to pressure sensitivity. *Biological Bulletin*, 1938, **75**, 357–359.
17. The perception of mechanical vibration: I. History of a controversy. *Journal of General Psychology*. 1940, **22**, 243–269.
18. The perception of mechanical vibration: II. The response of pressure receptors. *Journal of General Psychology*, 1940, **22**, 271–280.
19. The perception of mechanical vibration: III. The frequency function. *Journal of General Psychology*, 1940, **22**, 281–289.
20. The perception of mechanical vibration: IV. Is there a separate "vibratory sense?" *Journal of General Psychology*, 1940, **22**, 291–308.
21. (with H. H. Manchester, Jr.) Sleep motility in student pilots. *Psychological Bulletin*, 1941, **38**, 693.
22. Explanation in science. *American Scientist*, 1942, **30**, 202–211.

23. A *study of the sleep motility of student pilots.* Washington, D.C.: U.S. Dept. Commerce, 1947. Pp. 18. (CAA Research Division Reports, No. 28, 1944.)

24. *Psychological mission to the Philippines.* Privately reproduced, 1946. Also section by the same title in Report No. 2, pp. 289–304, of *The aviation psychology research program of the Army Air Forces: The classification program.* Washington, D.C.: U.S. Government Printing Office, 1947.

25. (with C. H. Harris) Selection and classification of air-crew by 'the Japanese. *American Psychologist,* 1946, **1**, 205–217.

26. Somesthesis. In E. G. Boring, H. S. Langfeld, & H. P. Weld (Eds.), *Foundations of psychology.* New York: Wiley, 1948. Pp. 360–379.

27. Somesthesis and the chemical senses. *Annual Review of Psychology,* 1950, **1**, 71–86.

28. Human resources aspects of the selection and classification of military manpower. In L. Carmichael & L. C. Mead (Eds.), *The selection of military manpower.* (Publ. No. 209) Washington, D.C.: National Academy of Sciences–National Research Council, 1951. Pp. 16–28.

29. The selection of pilots in the U.S. Air Force. In F. Baumgarten (Ed.), *La psychotechnique dans le monde moderne.* Paris: Presses Universitaires de France, 1952. Pp. 500–506.

30. *The human senses.* New York: Wiley; London: Chapman & Hall, 1953. x + 365 pp.

31. Military psychology: Science or technology? *American Journal of Psychology,* July, 1953, **66**(3), 335–348.

32. Hearing through the skin. *ONR Research Reviews,* October, 1954, 15–20.

33. The utilization of cutaneous reception for communications. *Proceedings of the Symposium on Physiological Psychology* (ONR Symposium Report ACR-1). Washington, D.C.: Navy Department, December, 1955.

34. Adventures in tactile literacy. *American Psychologist*, 1957, **12**, 115–124.

35. *Experimental psychology at Oxford, 1956.* (Technical Report ONRL-3-57). London: American Embassy, January 8, 1957.

36. *The study of perceptual illusions at Geneva.* (Technical Report ONRL-23-57) London: American Embassy, February 26, 1957.

37. *Recent developments in experimental psychology in Austria, Southern Germany, and Switzerland.* (Tech. Rep. ONRL-25-57) London: American Embassy, March 6, 1957.

38. (with D. M. Gates) *Institute of Optics, Paris.* (Technical Report ONRL-45-57) London: American Embassy, April 15, 1957.

39. *Military psychology in France.* (Tech. Rep. ONRL-56-57) London: American Embassy, May 27, 1957.

40. *St. Andrews symposium on engineering psychology.* (Technical Report ONRL-57-57) London: American Embassy, May 27, 1957.

41. *Italian psychophysiology and experimental psychology, 1957.* (Technical Report ONRL-80-57) London: American Embassy, July 9, 1957.

42. *Developments in Scandinavian psychology, 1957.* (Technical Report ONRL-92-57) London: American Embassy, July 29, 1957.

43. The first international symposium on military psychology. *American Psychologist*, 1957, **12**, 737–739.

44. Engineering psychology: a symposium of the British Psychological Society. *Occupational Psychology,* 1957, **3,** 1–9.
45. Cutaneous Sensation, Kinesthesis, Deep Pain, Pressure Sensitivity, etc. A group of 12 articles in *Encyclopedia of Science and Technology.* New York: McGraw-Hill, 1960.
46. Some neglected possibilities of communication. *Science,* 1960, **131,** 1583–1588.
47. Where is science taking us? (Contribution to the Research Frontier department). *Saturday Review,* July 2, 1960, 48–49.
48. *Proceedings of the first international symposium on military psychology.* (Coedited with M. C. Lee) Publication 894, Washington, D.C.: NAS–NRC, 1961.
49. Cutaneous channels of communication. In W. A. Rosenblith (Ed.), *Sensory communication.* New York: Wiley, 1961. Pp. 73–87.
50. A NATO symposium on defense psychology. *American Psychologist,* 1961, **16,** 320–325.
51. (Ed.) *Defense psychology.* (NATO Conference Series No. 1) London: Pergamon Press, 1962. vii + 354 pp.
52. *Fundamentals of psychology.* New York: Wiley, 1962. Foreword by E. G. Boring, 437 pp.
53. (Ed.) *Communication processes.* (NATO Conference Series No. 4) London: Pergamon Press, 1965. x + 299 pp.
54. Pattern perception by the skin. In D. R. Kenshalo (Ed.), *The skin senses.* Springfield, Illinois: Charles C Thomas, 1967. Pp. 304–321.
55. (with C. E. Sherrick) Multiple cutaneous stimulation: The discrimination of vibratory patterns.

Journal of the Acoustical Society of America, 1965, **37**, 797–801.

56. Cutaneous coding of optical signals: the optohapt. *Perception & Psychophysics,* 1966, **1**, 377–381.

57. *Fundamentos de psicología* (Translation, in Spanish, by L. L. Tapia, of *Fundamentals of psychology,* 1962), Mexico City: Trillas, 1968.

58. Body English. *Psychology Today,* Dec., 1968, 43–47; also reprinted in *Readings in Psychology Today* and in *Readings in Experimental Psychology Today.* Del Mar, California: CRM Books, 1969.

59. Vision, audition, and beyond. In W. D. Neff (Ed.), *Advances in sensory physiology,* Vol. 4. New York: Academic Press, 1970. Pp. 1–17.

60. *Handboek van de Psychologie.* (Translation, in Dutch, of *Fundamentals of psychology,* 1962). Amsterdam: Aula, 1970. 2 vols.

61. Cutaneous sensation, Headache, Itch, etc. Twelve brief articles in *Encyclopedia of science and technology.* (3rd ed.) New York: McGraw-Hill, 1971.

62. *Grondbeginsels van die Psigologie.* (Translation, in Afrikaans, by S. J. Prins of *Fundamentals of psychology,* 1962). Pretoria: Van Schaik, 1971. 451 pp.

63. Body English. In J. A. DeVito (Ed.), *Communication concepts and processes.* Englewood Cliffs, New Jersey: Prentice-Hall, 1971. Pp. 115–126.

64. *The human senses.* (2nd ed.) New York: Wiley, 1972. x + 584 pp.

65. *Psicofisiologia degli Organi de Senso.* (Translation of *The human senses,* 1972, by A. M. Longoni, G. B. Flores d'Arcais, L. Arcuri, & A. Mannucci). Milan: Martello, 1972. xii + 711 pp.

66. Reply to Festschrift. In Festschrift for Frank A. Geldard, Princeton University. *Psychonomic Monograph Supplements,* 1972, 4, 218–238.
67. Vision—from a wide mantel. (The Clarence H. Graham Memorial Lecture, Nov. 11, 1971, Psychonomic Society, St. Louis, Missouri). *Perception and Psychophysics,* 1972, 11, 193–197.
68. Clarence Henry Graham, 1906–1971. *American Journal of Psychology,* 1972, 85, 291–294.
69. Cutaneous coding of optical signals: the optohapt. In F. J. McGuigan & P. J. Woods (Eds.), *Contemporary studies in psychology.* New York: Appleton-Century-Crofts, 1972. Pp. 56–62.
70. (with C. E. Sherrick) The cutaneous "rabbit"; a perceptual illusion. *Science,* 1972, 178, 178–179.
71. Vibratory reception in hairy skin. In G. B. Flores d'Arcais (Ed.), *Festschrift for Fabio Metelli.* Milan: Martello, 1975. Pp. 301–311.
72. Tactile communication. In T. A. Sebeok (Ed.), *How animals communicate.* Bloomington, Indiana: Indiana University Press, 1975. Chapter 11.

Index

Variable in saltatory
    experiments (*contd.*)
distance between con-
    tactors as, 38–40
direction of pulse train
    as possible, 38, 113
frequency as possible,
    113
intensity as, 58–62, 111,
    113
irregularity of pulsing
    as, 40–41, 112–113
locus of stimulation as,
    38, 77, 113
number of contactors
    as, 36, 42–45
number of pulses as,
    36–38
size and shape as pos-
    sible, 109
temporal spacing of
    pulses as, 49 ff., 57,
    60, 72, 98
"tuning" (precondi-
    tioning) as, 41, 113
wave composition as
    possible, 113
Velocity of wave conduc-
    tion, 68–71
Vibration analyzer, 88
Vibratory matrix, 45
Virginia, University of, 9
Vision, as spatial sense,
    81–82

Visual fractionation, 95–
    98
Visual "persistence," 97
Visual preadaptation,
    99–100
Visual problems, 113–116
Visual saltation, 81, 89–
    116
central seat of, 106–107
von Békésy, G., 23, 25, 118
von Helmholtz, H. L. F.,
    7, 82, 91, 114, 118
von Kries, J., 114

W

Wave composition, as a
    possible variable, 113
Wave velocity, 68–71
of abdominal skin, 70
in forearm, 68–70
of shin, 60–71
of thigh, 70
White rabbit, 108
Wundt, W., 7, 12, 13

X

X–Y plotter, 68, 69

Y

Yellow rabbit, 108

Z

Zeppelins in Rockies, 18